Birds of California
Field Guide

by Stan Tekiela

ADVENTURE PUBLICATIONS, INC.
CAMBRIDGE, MINNESOTA

To my wife Katherine and daughter Abigail with all my love

ACKNOWLEDGMENTS:
Special thanks to the National Wildlife Refuge System, which stewards the land that is critical to many bird species. Special thanks also to Brian E. Small for reviewing the range maps.

Edited by Sandy Livoti; Range maps produced by Anthony Hertzel
Book design and illustrations by Jonathan Norberg

Photo credits by photographer and page number:
Cover photo: Male Western Bluebird by Stan Tekiela
Rick and Nora Bowers: 228 **Dominique Braud:** 378 (adult) **Brian M. Collins**: 210, 334 **Cornell Laboratory of Ornithology**: 96 (female), 288 (both) **Dudley Edmondson**: 14, 16, 18, 24, 26, 28, 30 (soaring), 36, 38 (both), 68, 74 (all), 102, 106, 110 (female), 118 (both), 122, 162 (both), 174, 180, 194 (perching), 218, 238 (non-breeding, in flight), 286 (male), 292 (female), 298 (perching, soaring), 300, 304 (winter, displaying), 308 (breeding, in flight, juvenile, in flight juvenile), 310, 362 (breeding, in flight), 364 (breeding), 366 (in flight) 368 (in flight, in flight juvenile), 386 (male, winter male), 388 (male), 392 (male), 402 **Don Enger**: 72 (rushing, weed dance) **B. Gerlach/DPA***: 344 (male) **Ned Harris**: 76 (soaring) **250** (juvenile) **Kevin T. Karlson**: 50, 54, 58, 64 (breeding), 142, 186 (both), 268, 294, 366 (breeding) **Bill Marchel**: 4, 96 (male), 100, 232 (female), 376 (in flight) **Steve and Dave Maslowski**: 8 (male), 44 (both), 46 (male), 80, 86, 90 (female), 116, 124, 144, 224, 240, 242, 258, 324 (male), 352 (male), 378 (chick-feeding adult), 396, 404 **Anthony Mercieca/DPA***: 344 (female) **Steve Mortensen**: 10, 66, 82, 84, 208, 386 **Warren Nelson**: 392 (female) **John Pennoyer**: 104, 336, 354 (male) **Brian E. Small**: 8 (female), 40, 46 (female), 52, 60, 64 (winter), 72 (breeding), 76 (perching), 88 (both), 90 (male), 92, 94 (both), 98, 110 (Oregon female), 112, 114, 128, 130, 134 (pale morph), 140 (winter) 166 (both), 168, 172, 176, 182 (breeding), 192, 196, 206, 212, 214 (male), 226 (both), 234 (perching), 238 (breeding, juvenile), 246 (non-breeding), 248, 254 (female), 256 (Oregon male), 264, 272, 274, 280, 282 (gray morph), 284, 290 (both), 296, 302, 308 (winter), 320 (both), 324 (female), 326 (both), 328, 330, 342 (female), 346, 348, 350, 352 (female), 354 (yellow male), 362 (winter), 364 (winter, juvenile), 366 (winter, juvenile), 368 (juvenile), 380 (female), 384 (female), 390, 394 (all), 398, 400 (both) **Stan Tekiela**: 2 (both), 6, 12, 20, 22, 30 (perching), 32 (both), 34 (both), 42 (both), 48 (breeding), 56, 62, 70, 72 (Clark's), 76 (juvenile), 78, 108, 120, 126 (both), 132, 134 (bottom), 136 (adult, 1 year old), 138, 140 (breeding), 146, 148, 150, 152, 154, 156 (all), 158, 160, 164, 170, 178, 184 (all), 188 (both), 190 (both),198, 200, 202, 204, 214 (female), 216, 222, 230, 232 (male), 236, 244, 246 (breeding), 250 (male, female), 252, 254 (male), 256 (male), 260, 262, 266, 270, 276, 278, 286 (female), 292 (male), 298 (juvenile), 312, 314 (both), 316 (both), 318 (both), 322 (both), 332, 338, 340, 342 (male), 356, 358, 360 (both), 364 (in flight), 368 (breeding), 370 (both), 372 (all), 374 (both), 376 (swimming, juvenile), 378 (in flight), 380 (male), 382 (both) 384 (male) **Brian K. Wheeler**: 194 (soaring), 220 (both), 234 (soaring, juvenile), 306 (all) **Jim Zipp**: 48 (winter), 136 (Bohemian), 282 (brown morph), 388 (female)
*Dembinsky Photo Associates

To the best of the publisher's knowledge, all photos were of live birds.

10 9 8 7 6 5 4
Copyright 2003 by Stan Tekiela
Published by Adventure Publications, Inc.
820 Cleveland St. S
Cambridge, MN 55008
1-800-678-7006
www.adventurepublications.net
All rights reserved
Printed in China
ISBN-13: 978-1-59193-031-0
ISBN-10: 1-59193-031-6

TABLE OF CONTENTS

Introduction

Sample Page

The Birds

Helpful Resources

Check List/Index

About the Author

WHY WATCH BIRDS IN CALIFORNIA?

Millions of people have discovered bird feeding. It's a simple and enjoyable way to bring the beauty of birds closer to your home. Watching birds at your feeder often leads to a lifetime pursuit of bird identification. The *Birds of California Field Guide* is for those who want to identify the common birds of California.

There are over 800 bird species in North America. In California alone there have been over 500 different kinds of birds recorded throughout the years. These bird sightings were documented by hundreds of bird watchers and became a part of the official state record. From these valuable records, I've chosen 170 of the most common birds of California to include in this field guide.

Bird watching, or birding, is the most popular spectator sport in America. Its appeal in California is due, in part, to an unusually rich and abundant birdlife. Why are there so many birds? One reason is open space. California is the third largest state, with more than 158,000 square miles (410,800 sq. km) and about 33 million people. On average, that is only 221 people per square mile (85 per sq. km). Most are located in southern California.

Open space is not the only reason there is such an abundance of birds. It's also the diversity of habitat. California can be broken into four distinctive habitats—the Pacific Border Province, Sierra-Cascade Province, Basin and Range Province and Lower California Province—each of which supports different groups of birds.

The Pacific Border Province, or Coastal Uplands, extends nearly the entire length of the coast along western California. Many of California's residents live here. This mainly mountainous region has many ridges, large valleys and several ranges, with elevations reaching 9,000 feet (2,750 m). This is a good place to see birds such as the California Towhee.

The Sierra-Cascade Province is a vast region that extends from Oregon to southern California. Located east of the Pacific Border, it is a belt of rugged mountain ranges with high peaks and deep valleys. Mount Whitney, the highest peak in the U.S. outside of

Alaska, is in this province. This region is heavily forested and is a good place to see Clark's Nutcrackers and Steller's Jays.

To the east of the Sierra-Cascade Province is the Basin and Range Province. Most of this region is flat, dry and sparsely vegetated, with low elevation deserts such as Death Valley and the Sonoran Desert. Usually receiving less than 2 inches (5 cm) of rainfall per year, this province is home to many wonderful birds such as Black-throated Sparrows and various hummingbirds species.

The Lower California Province is in most of the southern part of the state. With its rolling mountains and valleys, it's a good place to see the California Gnatcatcher, a species of special concern.

Water also plays a big part in California's bird populations. There are 840 miles (1,352 km) of coastline, with a total of 3,427 miles (5,517 km) of coast including all the inlets and islands. The coast is a great place to see many gull species such as California Gull or Heermann's Gull. California also has over 2,675 square miles (6,950 sq. km) of fresh water surface. The Sacramento and San Joaquin Rivers are the largest, and several drain the entire state. There are also several thousand small lakes. Salton Sea and Lake Tahoe are the largest and are home to birds such as American Avocets and American White Pelicans. It's always worth time to investigate bodies of water in California for the presence of birds.

Varying habitats in California also mean variations in weather. California has the highest and lowest elevations in the lower 48 states, rising from 282 feet (86 m) below sea level in Death Valley to 14,494 feet (4,419 m) at Mount Whitney. Northern parts of California are cooler and moister than southern California. The Mojave Desert is the hottest region in California and the U.S. in the summer, while winters in the mountains are cold and snowy with many snowcapped peaks year-round.

No matter if you're in the hot, arid deserts or in the cool, moist mountains of California, there are birds to watch in each season. Whether witnessing hawks migrating in autumn or welcoming back hummingbirds in spring, there is variety and excitement in birding as each season turns to the next.

OBSERVE WITH A STRATEGY; TIPS FOR IDENTIFYING BIRDS

Identifying birds isn't as difficult as you might think. By simply following a few basic strategies, you can increase your chances of successfully identifying most birds you see! One of the first and easiest things to do when you see a new bird is to note its color. (Also, since this book is organized by color, you will go right to that color section to find it.)

Next, note the size of the bird. A strategy to quickly estimate size is to select a small-, medium- and large-sized bird to use for reference. For example, most people are familiar with robins. A robin, measured from tip of the bill to tip of the tail, is 10 inches (25 cm) long. Using the robin as an example of a medium-sized bird, select two other birds, one smaller and one larger. Many people use a House Sparrow, at about 6 inches (15 cm), and an American Crow, about 18 inches (45 cm). When you see a bird that you don't know, you can quickly ask yourself, "Is it smaller than a robin, but larger than a sparrow?" When you look in your field guide to help identify your bird, you'll know it's roughly between 6-10 inches (15-25 cm) long. This will help to narrow your choices.

Next, note the size, shape and color of the bill. Is it long, short, thick, thin, pointed, blunt, curved or straight? Seed-eating birds, such as the Blue Grosbeak, have bills that are thick and strong enough to crack even the toughest seeds. Birds that sip nectar, such as Black-chinned Hummingbirds, need long thin bills to reach deep into flowers. Hawks and owls tear their prey with very sharp, curving bills. Sometimes, just noting the bill shape can help you decide if the bird is a woodpecker, finch, grosbeak, blackbird or bird of prey.

Next, take a look around and note the habitat in which you see the bird. Is it wading in a saltwater marsh? Walking along a riverbank or on the beach? Soaring in the sky? Is it perched high in the trees or hopping along the forest floor? Because of their preferences in diet and habitat, you'll usually see robins hopping on the ground, but not often eating seeds at a feeder. Or you will see a Blue Grosbeak sitting on the branches of a tree, but not climbing down the tree trunk headfirst the way a nuthatch does.

Noticing what a bird is eating will give you another clue to help you identify that bird. Feeding is a big part of any bird's life. Fully one-third of all bird activity revolves around searching for and catching food, or actually eating. While birds don't always follow all the rules of what we think they eat, you can make some general assumptions. Northern Flickers, for instance, feed upon ants and other insects, so you wouldn't expect to see them visiting a backyard feeder. Some birds, such as Barn Swallows and Cliff Swallows, feed upon flying insects, and spend hours swooping and diving to catch a meal.

Sometimes you can identify a bird by the way it perches. Body posture can help you differentiate between an American Crow and a Red-tailed Hawk. American Crows lean forward over their feet on a branch, while hawks perch in a vertical position. Look for this the next time you see a large unidentified bird in a tree.

Birds in flight are often difficult to identify, but noting the size and shape of the wing will help. A bird's wing size is in direct proportion to its body size, weight and type of flying. The shape of the wing determines if the bird flies fast and with precision, or slowly and less precisely. Birds such as House Finches, which flit around in thick tangles of branches, have short round wings. Birds that soar on warm updrafts of air, such as Turkey Vultures, have long broad wings. Barn Swallows have short pointed wings that slice through air, propelling their swift and accurate flight.

Some birds have unique flight patterns that aid in identification. American Goldfinches fly in a distinctive up-and-down pattern that makes it look as if they are riding a roller coaster.

While it's not easy to make these observations in the short time you often have to watch a "mystery bird," practicing these methods of identification will greatly expand your skills in birding. Also, seek the guidance of a more experienced birder who will help you improve your skills and answer questions on the spot.

BIRD BASICS

It's easier to identify birds and communicate about them if you know the names of the different parts of a bird. For instance, it's more effective to use the word "crest" to indicate the set of extra long feathers on top of the head of a Steller's Jay than to try to describe it.

The following illustration points out the basic parts of a bird. Because it is a composite of many birds, it shouldn't be confused with any actual bird.

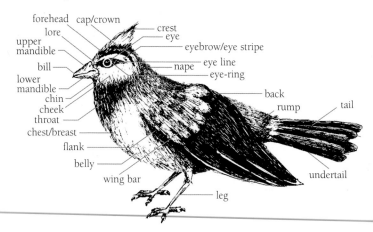

BIRD COLOR VARIABLES

No other animal has a color pallet like a bird's. Brilliant blues, lemon yellows, showy reds and iridescent greens are common-place within the bird world. In general, the male birds are more colorful than their female counterparts. This is probably to help the male attract a mate, essentially saying, "Hey, look at me!" It also calls attention to the male's overall health. The better the condition of his feathers, the better his food source and territory, and therefore the better his potential for a mate.

Female birds that don't look like their male counterparts (such species are called sexually dimorphic, meaning "two forms") are often a nondescript color, as seen with the Lazuli Bunting. These muted tones help hide the females during weeks of motionless incubation, and draw less attention to them when they are out feeding or taking a break from the rigors of raising their young.

In some species, such as the Bald Eagle, Steller's Jay and Hairy Woodpecker, the male birds look nearly identical to the females. In the case of the woodpeckers, the sexes are only differentiated by a single red or sometimes yellow mark. Depending on the species, the mark may be on top of the head, face, nape of the neck or just behind the bill.

During the first year, juvenile birds often look like the mothers. Since brightly colored feathers are used mainly for attracting a mate, young non-breeding males don't have a need for colorful plumage. It is not until the first spring molt (or several years later, depending on the species) that young males obtain their breeding colors.

Both breeding and winter plumages are the result of molting. Molting is the process of dropping old worn feathers and replacing them with new ones. All birds molt, typically twice a year, with the spring molt usually occurring in late winter. During this time, most birds produce their breeding plumage (brighter colors for attracting mates), which lasts throughout the summer.

Winter plumage is the result of the late summer molt, which serves a couple of important functions. First, it adds feathers for warmth in the coming winter. Second, in some species it produces feathers that tend to be drab in color, which helps to camouflage the birds and hide them from predators. The winter plumage of the male American Goldfinch, for example, is an olive brown unlike its obvious canary yellow color in summer. Luckily for us, some birds, such as Lewis's Woodpeckers, retain their bright summer colors all year long.

BIRD NESTS

Bird nests are truly an amazing feat of engineering. Imagine building your home strong enough to weather a storm, large enough to hold your entire family, insulated enough to shelter them from cold and heat, and waterproof enough to keep out rain. Now, build it without any blueprints or directions, and without the use of your hands or feet! Birds do!

Before building a nest, an appropriate site must be selected. In some species, such as House Wrens, the male picks out several potential sites and assembles several small twigs in each. This discourages other birds from using nearby nest cavities. These "extra" nests are occasionally called dummy nests. The female is then taken around and shown all the choices. She chooses her favorite and finishes constructing the nest. In some other species of birds–the Bullock's Oriole, for example–it is the female who chooses the site and builds the nest with the male offering only an occasional suggestion. Each species has its own nest-building routine, which is strictly followed.

Nesting material usually consists of natural elements found in the immediate area. Most nests consist of plant fibers (such as bark peeled from grapevines), sticks, mud, dried grass, feathers, fur, or soft fuzzy tufts from thistle. Some birds, including Black-chinned Hummingbirds, use spider webs to glue nest materials together. Nesting material is limited to what a bird can hold or carry. Because of this, a bird must make many trips afield to gather enough materials to complete its nest. Most nests take at least four days or more, and hundreds, if not thousands, of trips to build.

As you'll see in the following illustrations, birds build a wide variety of nest types.

| **ground nest** | **platform nest** | **cup nest** | **pendulous nest** | **cavity nest** |

The simple **ground nest** is scraped out of the earth. A shallow depression that usually contains no nesting material, it is made by birds such as the Killdeer and Horned Lark.

Another kind of nest, the **platform nest**, represents a more complex type of nest building. Constructed of small twigs and branches, the platform nest is a simple arrangement of sticks which forms a platform and features a small depression to nestle the eggs.

Some platform nests, such as those of the Canada Goose, are constructed on the ground and are made with mud and grass. Platform nests can also be on cliffs, bridges, balconies or even in flowerpots. This kind of nest gives space to adventurous youngsters and functions as a landing platform for the parents. Many waterfowl construct platform nests on the ground, usually near water or actually in the water. These floating platform nests vary with the water level, thus preventing nests with eggs from being flooded. Platform nests, constructed by such birds as Mourning Doves and herons, are not anchored to the tree and may tumble from the branches during high winds and storms.

The **cup nest** is a modified platform nest, used by three-quarters of all songbirds. Constructed from the outside in, a supporting platform is constructed first. This platform is attached firmly to a tree, shrub, rock ledge or the ground. Next, the sides are constructed of grasses, small twigs, bark or leaves, which are woven together and often glued with mud for additional strength. The inner cup, lined with feathers, animal fur, soft plant material or animal hair, is constructed last. The mother bird uses her chest to cast the final contours of the inner nest.

The **pendulous nest** is an unusual nest, looking more like a sock hanging from a branch than a nest. Inaccessible to most predators, these nests are attached to the ends of the smallest branches of a tree, and often wave wildly in the breeze. Woven very tightly of plant fibers, they are strong and watertight, taking up to a week to build. More commonly used by tropical birds, this complicated nest type has also been mastered by orioles and kinglets. A small opening on the top or side allows the parents access to the grass-lined interior. (It must be one heck of a ride to be inside one of these nests during a windy spring thunderstorm!)

Another type of nest, the **cavity nest**, is used by many birds, including woodpeckers and Western Bluebirds. The cavity nest is usually excavated in a tree branch or trunk and offers shelter from storms, sun, predators and cold. A relatively small entrance hole in a tree leads to an inner chamber up to 10 inches (25 cm) below. Usually constructed by woodpeckers, the cavity nest is typically used only once by its builder, but subsequently can be used for many years by birds such as Wood Ducks, mergansers and bluebirds, which do not have the capability of excavating one for themselves. Kingfishers, on the other hand, excavate a tunnel up to 4 feet (1 m) long, which connects the entrance in a riverbank to the nest chamber. These cavity nests are often sparsely lined because they are already well insulated.

Some birds, including some swallows, take nest building one step further. They use a collection of small balls of mud to construct an adobe-style home. Constructed beneath the eaves of houses, under bridges or inside chimneys, some of these nests look like simple cup nests. Others are completely enclosed, with small tunnel-like openings that lead into a safe nesting chamber for the baby birds.

One of the most clever of all nest types is known as the **no nest** or daycare nest. Parasitic birds, such as Brown-headed Cowbirds, build no nests at all! The egg-laden female expertly searches out other birds' nests and sneaks in to lay one of her own eggs while the host mother is not looking, thereby leaving the host mother to raise an adopted youngster. The mother cowbird wastes no energy building a nest only to have it raided by a predator. By using several nests of other birds, she spreads out her progeny so at least one of her offspring will live to maturity.

WHO BUILDS THE NEST?

In general, the female bird builds the nest. She gathers nesting materials and constructs a nest, with an occasional visit from her mate to check on the progress. In some species, both parents contribute equally to the construction of a nest. A male bird might forage for precisely the right sticks, grass or mud, but it's often the female that forms or puts together the nest. She uses her body to form the egg chamber. Rarely does the male build a nest by himself.

FLEDGING

Fledging is the interval between hatching and flight or leaving the nest. Some birds leave the nest within hours of hatching (precocial), but it might be weeks before they are able to fly. This is common with waterfowl and shorebirds. Until they start to fly, they are called fledglings. Birds that are still in the nest are called nestlings. Other baby birds are born naked and blind, and remain in the nest for several weeks (altricial).

WHY BIRDS MIGRATE

Why do birds migrate? The short answer is simple—food. Birds migrate to areas with high concentrations of food, as it is easier to breed where food is than where it is not. A typical migrating bird—the Western Tanager, for instance—will migrate from the tropics of Central America and Mexico to nest in forests of North America, taking advantage of billions of newly hatched insects to feed its young. This trip is called **complete migration**.

Some birds of prey return from their complete migration to northern regions that are overflowing with small rodents, such as mice and voles, that have continued to breed in winter.

Complete migrators have a set time and pattern of migration. Each year at nearly the same time, they take off and head for a specific wintering ground. Complete migrators may travel great distances, sometimes as much as 15,000 miles (24,150 km) or more in a year. But complete migration doesn't necessarily imply flying from the cold, frozen northland to a tropical destination. The Black-chinned Hummingbird, for example, is a complete migrator that flies from California to spend the winter in Central and South America. This is still called complete migration.

There are many interesting aspects to complete migrators. In the spring, males usually migrate several weeks before the females, arriving early to scope out possibilities for nesting sites and food sources, and to begin to defend territories. The females arrive several weeks later. In the autumn, in many species, the females and their young leave early, often up to four weeks before the adult males.

All migrators are not the same type. There are **partial migrators**, such as Lesser Goldfinches, that usually wait until food supplies dwindle before flying south. Unlike complete migrators, partial migrators move only far enough south, or sometimes east and west, to find abundant food. In some years it might be only a few hundred miles. In other years it might be nearly a thousand. This kind of migration, dependent on the weather and available food, is sometimes called **seasonal movement**.

Unlike the predictable ebbing and flowing behavior of complete migrators or partial migrators, **irruptive migrators** can move every third to fifth year or, in some cases, in consecutive years. These migrations are triggered when times are really tough and food is scarce. Red-breasted Nuthatches are a good example of irruptive migrators, because they leave their normal northern range in search of food or in response to overpopulation.

How Do Birds Migrate?

One of the many secrets of migration is fat. While we humans are fighting the battle of the bulge, birds intentionally gorge themselves to put on as much fat as possible while still being able to fly. Fat provides the greatest amount of energy per unit of weight, and in the same way that your car needs gas, birds are propelled by fat and stalled without it.

During long migratory flights, fat deposits are used up quickly, and birds need to stop to "refuel." This is when backyard bird feeding stations and undeveloped, natural spaces around our towns and cities are especially important. Some birds require up to 2-3 days of constant feeding to build their fat reserves before continuing their seasonal trip.

Some birds, such as most eagles, hawks, falcons and vultures, migrate during the day. Larger birds can hold more body fat, go longer without eating and take longer to migrate. These birds glide on rising columns of warm air, called thermals, which hold them aloft while they slowly make their way north or south. They generally rest during nights and hunt early in the morning before the sun has a chance to warm up the land and create good soaring conditions. Birds migrating during the day use a combination of landforms, rivers, and the rising and setting sun to guide them in the right direction.

Most other birds migrate during the night. Studies show that some birds which migrate at night use the stars to navigate. Others use the setting sun, while still others, such as doves, use the earth's magnetic fields to guide them north or south. While flying at night might seem like a crazy idea, nocturnal migration is safer for several reasons. First, there are fewer nighttime predators for migrating birds. Second, traveling at night allows time during the day to find food in unfamiliar surroundings. Finally, nighttime wind patterns tend to be flat, or laminar. These flat winds don't have the turbulence associated with daytime winds and can actually help carry smaller birds by pushing them along.

HOW TO USE THIS GUIDE

To help you quickly and easily identify birds, this book is organized by color. Simply note the color of the bird and turn to that section. Refer to the first page for the color key. The Williamson's Sapsucker, for example, is black and white with a yellow belly. Because the bird is mostly black and white, it will be found in the black and white section. Each color section is also arranged by size, generally with the smaller birds first. Sections may also incorporate the average size in a range, which, in some cases, reflects size differences between the male and female birds. Flip through the pages in that color section to find the bird. If you already know the name of the bird, check the index for the page number. In some species, the male and female are remarkably different in color. In others, the color of the breeding and winter plumages differs. These species have an inset photograph with a page reference and in most cases are found in two color sections.

In the description section you will find a variety of information about the bird. On the next page is a sample of the information included in the book.

RANGE MAPS

Range maps are included for each bird. Colored areas indicate where in California a particular bird is most likely to be found. The colors represent the presence of a species during a specific season, not the density or amount of birds in the area. Green is used for summer, blue for winter, red for year-round and yellow for areas where the bird is seen during migration. While every effort has been made to accurately depict these ranges, they are only general guidelines. Ranges actually change on an ongoing basis due to a variety of factors. Changes in weather, species abundance, landscape and vital resources such as the availability of food and water can affect local populations, migration and movements, causing birds to be found in areas that are atypical for the species.

Colored areas simply mean bird sightings for that species have been frequent in those areas and less frequent in the others. Please use the maps as intended–as general guides only.

COMMON NAME
Scientific name

YEAR-ROUND
MIGRATION
SUMMER
WINTER

Size: measures head to tail, may include wingspan

Male: a brief description of the male bird, and may include breeding, winter or other plumages

Female: a brief description of the female bird, which is sometimes not the same as the male

Juvenile: a brief description of the juvenile bird, which often looks like the female

Nest: the kind of nest this bird builds to raise its young; who builds the nest; how many broods per year

Eggs: how many eggs you might expect to see in a nest; color and marking

Incubation: the average time parents spend incubating the eggs; who does the incubation

Fledging: the average time young spend in the nest after hatching but before they leave the nest; who does the most "childcare" and feeding

Migration: complete (consistent, seasonal), partial migrator (seasonal, destination varies), irruptive (unpredictable, depends on the food supply), non-migrator; additional comments

Food: what the bird eats most of the time (e.g., seeds, insects, fruit, nectar, small mammals, fish); if it typically comes to a bird feeding station

Compare: notes about other birds that look similar, and the pages on which they can be found

Stan's Notes: Interesting gee-whiz natural history information. This could be something to look or listen for, or something to help positively identify the bird. Also includes remarkable features.

winter

breeding

EUROPEAN STARLING
Sturnus vulgaris

Size: 7½" (19 cm)

Male: Gray-to-black bird with white speckles in fall and winter. Shiny purple black during spring and summer. Long, pointed yellow bill in spring turns gray in fall. Short tail.

Female: same as male

Juvenile: similar to adult, gray brown in color with a streaked chest

Nest: cavity; male and female line cavity; 2 broods per year

Eggs: 4-6; bluish with brown markings

Incubation: 12-14 days; female and male incubate

Fledging: 18-20 days; female and male feed young

Migration: non-migrator

Food: insects, seeds, fruit; comes to seed and suet feeders

Compare: The male Brown-headed Cowbird (pg. 5) is the same size, but has a brown head and longer tail.

Stan's Notes: A great songster, this bird can also mimic sounds. Often displaces woodpeckers, chickadees and other cavity-nesting birds. Can be very aggressive and destroy eggs or young of other birds. The bill changes color with the seasons: yellow in spring and gray in autumn. Jaws are designed to be the most powerful when opening, as they pry open crevices to locate hidden insects. Gathers in the hundreds in autumn. Not a native bird, it was introduced to New York City in 1890-91 from Europe.

female pg. 139

male

BROWN-HEADED COWBIRD
Molothrus ater

**YEAR-ROUND
SUMMER**

Size: 7½" (19 cm)

Male: A glossy black bird, reminiscent of a Red-winged Blackbird. Chocolate brown head with a pointed, sharp gray bill.

Female: dull brown bird with bill similar to male

Juvenile: similar to female, only dull gray color and a streaked chest

Nest: no nest; lays eggs in nests of other birds

Eggs: 5-7; white with brown markings

Incubation: 10-13 days; host bird incubates eggs

Fledging: 10-11 days; host birds feed young

Migration: non-migrator to partial in California

Food: insects, seeds; will come to seed feeders

Compare: The male Red-winged Blackbird (pg. 11) is slightly larger with red and yellow patches on upper wings. European Starling (pg. 3) has a shorter tail.

Stan's Notes: A member of the blackbird family. Of approximately 750 species of parasitic birds worldwide, this is the only parasitic bird in the state, laying eggs in host birds' nests, leaving others to raise its young. Cowbirds are known to have laid eggs in nests of over 200 species of birds. Some birds reject cowbird eggs, but most incubate them and raise the young, even to the exclusion of their own. Look for warblers and other birds feeding young birds twice their own size. At one time cowbirds followed bison to feed on insects attracted to the animals.

male

female
pg. 277

PHAINOPEPLA
Phainopepla nitens

YEAR-ROUND SUMMER

Size: 8" (20 cm)

Male: Slim, long, glossy black bird with a ragged crest and deep red eyes. Wing patches near tips of wings are white, obvious in flight.

Female: slim, long, mostly gray bird with a ragged crest and deep red eyes, whitish wing bars

Juvenile: similar to female

Nest: cup; female and male construct; 1-2 broods per year

Eggs: 2-4; gray with brown markings

Incubation: 12-14 days; female and male incubate

Fledging: 18-20 days; female and male feed young

Migration: complete, to California and Arizona

Food: fruit (usually mistletoe), insects; will come to water elements or water drips in yards

Compare: The only all-black bird with a crest and red eyes. Look for white wing patches in flight.

Stan's Notes: Seen in desert scrub with water and mistletoe nearby. Gives a low, liquid "kweer" song, but will also mimic other species. In winter individuals defend food supply such as a single tree with abundant mistletoe berries. Probably responsible for the dispersal of mistletoe plants far and wide. Male will fly up to a height of 300 feet (90 m), circling and zigzagging to court female. Builds nest of twigs and plant fibers and binds it with spider webs in the crotch of a mistletoe cluster. Lines nest with hair or soft plant fibers. May be the only species to nest in two regions in the same nest season. Nests in dry desert habitat in early spring. When it gets hot, moves to a higher area with an abundant water supply to nest again.

male

female

SPOTTED TOWHEE
Pipilo maculatus

YEAR-ROUND WINTER

Size: 8½" (22 cm)

Male: A mostly black bird with dirty red-brown sides and white belly. Multiple white spots on wings and sides. Long black tail with a white tip. Rich red eyes.

Female: very similar to male, with a brown head

Juvenile: brown with a heavily streaked chest

Nest: cup; female builds; 1-2 broods per year

Eggs: 3-5; white with brown markings

Incubation: 12-14 days; female and male incubate

Fledging: 10-12 days; female and male feed young

Migration: non-migrator to partial migrator

Food: seeds, fruit, insects

Compare: Closely related to the Green-tailed Towhee (pg. 329), which lacks Spotted's bold black and red colors. California Towhee (pg. 155) is larger and lacks rusty red sides.

Stan's Notes: Found in a variety of habitats, from thick brush and chaparral to suburban backyards. Usually heard noisily scratching through dead leaves on the ground for food. Over 70 percent of its diet is plant material. Eats more insects during spring and summer. Well known for retreating from danger by walking away rather than taking to flight. Nest is nearly always on the ground under bushes, but away from where the male perches to sing. Begins breeding in April. Lays eggs in May. After the breeding season, moves to higher elevations. Song and plumage vary geographically and are not well studied or understood.

9

female pg. 149

male

RED-WINGED BLACKBIRD
Agelaius phoeniceus

Size: 8½" (22 cm)

Male: Jet black bird with red and yellow shoulder patches on upper wings. Pointed black bill.

Female: heavily streaked brown bird with a pointed brown bill and white eyebrows

Juvenile: same as female

Nest: cup; female builds; 2-3 broods per year

Eggs: 3-4; bluish green with brown markings

Incubation: 10-12 days; female incubates

Fledging: 11-14 days; female and male feed young

Migration: non-migrator to partial migrator

Food: seeds, insects; will come to seed feeders

Compare: The male Tricolored Blackbird (pg. 13) has red and white shoulder patches (epaulets). The male Brown-headed Cowbird (pg. 5) is slightly smaller, more iridescent and has a brown head.

Stan's Notes: One of the most widespread and numerous birds in the state. It is a sure sign of spring when the Red-winged Blackbirds return to the marshes. Flocks of up to 100,000 birds have been reported. Males return before the females and defend territories by singing from tops of surrounding vegetation. Males repeat call from the tops of cattails while showing off their red and yellow wing bars (epaulets). Females choose mate and usually will nest over shallow water in thick stands of cattails. Red-wingeds feed mostly on seeds in fall and spring, switching to insects during summer.

male

female pg. 151

YEAR-ROUND

Size: 9" (22.5 cm)

Male: Black with red and white shoulder patches (epaulets). Pointed dark bill and very dark reddish brown eyes.

Female: overall dark brown, gray chin and breast, pointed dark bill, black legs, dark reddish brown eyes

Juvenile: similar to female, but not as brown

Nest: cup; female builds; 2 broods per year

Eggs: 3-4; pale green with brown markings

Incubation: 11-13 days; female incubates

Fledging: 11-14 days; female and male feed young

Migration: non-migrator to partial migrator; will move around to find food

Food: insects, seeds, grain; visits ground feeders

Compare: The male Red-winged Blackbird (pg. 11) is similar, but has red and yellow epaulets.

Stan's Notes: Blackbird species found mainly in California. Very closely related to Red-winged Blackbirds. Tricolored usually has a smaller bill than Red-winged. Flocks with Red-wingeds and other blackbirds during winter, moving around to find food and nesting colonies. Sometimes moves from one area to another for unknown reasons. Tricoloreds and Red-wingeds have some of the highest nesting densities of any bird species, with some colonies in the tens of thousands. Like the Red-winged, it nests in shallow freshwater marshes. Builds nest from woven sedges, grasses and other green plants. Attaches nest to upright cattail stems and lines it with finer plant fibers. Young are fed mainly insects.

female pg. 153

male

BREWER'S BLACKBIRD
Euphagus cyanocephalus

YEAR-ROUND
SUMMER
WINTER

Size: 9" (22.5 cm)

Male: Overall glossy black, shining green in direct light. Head more purple than green. Bright white or pale yellow eyes. Winter plumage can be dull gray to black.

Female: similar to male, only overall grayish brown, most have dark eyes

Juvenile: similar to female

Nest: cup; female builds; 1-2 broods per year

Eggs: 4-6; gray with brown markings

Incubation: 12-14 days; female incubates

Fledging: 13-14 days; female and male feed young

Migration: non-migrator to partial in California; moves around to find food

Food: insects, seeds, fruit

Compare: Smaller than the male Great-tailed Grackle (pg. 25), lacking the long tail. Male Brown-headed Cowbird (pg. 5) is smaller and has a brown head. Male Red-winged Blackbird (pg. 11) has red and yellow shoulder marks.

Stan's Notes: Common blackbird often found in association with agricultural lands and seen in open areas such as wet pastures and mountain meadows up to 10,000 feet (3,050 m). Male and some females are easily identified by their bright, nearly white eyes. It is a common cowbird host, usually nesting in a shrub, small tree or directly on the ground. Prefers to nest in small colonies of up to 20 pairs. Gathers in large flocks with cowbirds, Red-wingeds and other blackbirds to migrate. It is expanding its range in North America.

female
pg. 161

male

YELLOW-HEADED BLACKBIRD
Xanthocephalus xanthocephalus

Size: 9-11" (22.5-28 cm)

Male: Large black bird with a lemon yellow head, chest and nape of neck. Black mask and a gray bill. White wing patches.

Female: similar to male, only slightly smaller with a brown body, dull yellow head and chest

Juvenile: similar to female

Nest: cup; female builds; 2 broods per year

Eggs: 3-5; greenish white with brown markings

Incubation: 11-13 days; female incubates

Fledging: 9-12 days; female feeds young

Migration: complete, to parts of California, Mexico

Food: insects, seeds; will come to ground feeders

Compare: Larger than the male Red-winged Blackbird (pg. 11), which has red and yellow patches on its wings. Male Yellow-headed Blackbird is the only large black bird with a bright yellow head.

Stan's Notes: Usually heard before seen, Yellow-headed Blackbird has a low, hoarse, raspy or metallic call. Nests in deep water marshes unlike its cousin, the Red-winged Blackbird, which prefers shallow water. The male gives an impressive mating display, flying with head drooped and feet and tail pointing down while steadily beating its wings. The female incubates alone and feeds 3-5 young. Young keep low and out of sight for as many as three weeks before starting to fly. Migrates in flocks of up to 200 with other blackbirds. Flocks made up mainly of males return first in early April; females return later. Most colonies consist of 20-100 nests.

COMMON MOORHEN
Gallinula chloropus

YEAR-ROUND
WINTER

Size: 14" (36 cm)

Male: Nearly black overall with yellow-tipped red bill. Red forehead. Thin line of white along sides. Yellowish green legs.

Female: same as male

Juvenile: same as adult, but brown with white throat and dirty yellow legs

Nest: ground; female and male build; 1-2 broods per year

Eggs: 2-10; brown with dark markings

Incubation: 19-22 days; female and male incubate

Fledging: 40-50 days; female and male feed young

Migration: non-migrator to partial in California

Food: insects, snails, seeds

Compare: Similar size as the American Coot (pg. 21), which lacks the distinctive yellow-tipped bill and red forehead of Moorhen.

Stan's Notes: Also known as Mud Hen or Pond Chicken. A nearly all-black duck-like bird often seen in freshwater marshes and lakes. Walks on floating vegetation or swims while hunting for insects. Females known to lay eggs in other moorhen nests in addition to their own. Sometimes takes old nest in a low shrub. A cooperative breeder, having young of first brood help raise young of second. Young leave nest usually within a few hours after hatching, but stay with the family for a couple months. Young ride on backs of adults.

YEAR-ROUND

AMERICAN COOT
Fulica americana

Size: 13-16" (33-40 cm)

Male: Slate gray to black all over, white bill with dark band near tip. Green legs and feet. A small white patch near the base of the tail. Prominent red eyes, with a small red patch above bill between eyes.

Female: same as male

Juvenile: much paler than adult, with a gray bill and same white rump patch

Nest: cup; female and male build; 1 brood per year

Eggs: 9-12; pinkish buff with brown markings

Incubation: 21-25 days; female and male incubate

Fledging: 49-52 days; female and male feed young

Migration: non-migrator in California

Food: insects, aquatic plants

Compare: Smaller than most waterfowl, it is the only black water bird or duck-like bird with a white bill.

Stan's Notes: An excellent diver and swimmer, often seen in large flocks on open water. Not a duck, as it doesn't have webbed feet, but instead has large lobed toes. When taking off, scrambles across surface of water with wings flapping. Bobs head while swimming. Floating nests are anchored to vegetation. Huge flocks of up to 1,000 birds gather for migration and during winter. The unusual name is of unknown origin, but in Middle English, *coote* was used to describe various waterfowl–perhaps it stuck. Like the Common Moorhen, American Coot is also called Mud Hen.

BLACK OYSTERCATCHER
Haematopus bachmani

YEAR-ROUND
WINTER

Size: 18" (45 cm)

Male: An overall black body with a bright reddish orange, heavy straight bill. Yellow eyes with a red outline. Yellow legs and feet. Stocky body with a short tail and broad wings, as seen in flight.

Female: same as male

Juvenile: similar to adult, with light brown body and dull orange, black-tipped bill

Nest: ground; female and male construct; 1 brood per year

Eggs: 1-3; dull white to olive with brown marks

Incubation: 24-29 days; female incubates

Fledging: 35-40 days; female and male feed young

Migration: non-migrator to partial in California

Food: insects, mollusks, worms, crustaceans

Compare: Avocet (pg. 65) has longer legs and a black and white body. The breeding Black-bellied Plover (pg. 51) has white on the head and a black and white back. Look for the stocky body and red-orange bill of Oystercatcher.

Stan's Notes: A shorebird found mainly along rocky shores. Rarely seen away from coast. Often alone and not approachable. Common name comes from its ability to feed on oysters and mussels. Uses its large bill to pry or sometimes chisel shells open with hammer-like blows. Believed to have a long-term pair bond. A noisy courtship display with much mutual bowing. Nest is a scrape on the ground, sometimes lined with shells and rocks, built above the high tide.

female pg. 181

male

GREAT-TAILED GRACKLE
Quiscalus mexicanus

YEAR-ROUND

Size: 18" (45 cm), male
15" (38 cm), female

Male: A large all-black bird with iridescent purple sheen on the head and back. Exceptionally long tail. Bright yellow eyes.

Female: considerably smaller than the male, overall brown bird with gray-to-brown belly, light brown-to-white eyes, eyebrows, throat and upper chest

Juvenile: similar to female

Nest: cup; female builds; 1-2 broods per year

Eggs: 3-5; greenish blue with brown markings

Incubation: 12-14 days; female incubates

Fledging: 21-23 days; female feeds young

Migration: non-migrator to partial in California; moves around to find food

Food: insects, fruit, seeds; comes to seed feeders

Compare: Male Brown-headed Cowbird (pg. 5) lacks the long tail and has a brown head.

Stan's Notes: This is our largest grackle. It was once considered a subspecies of the Boat-tailed Grackle, which occurs along the East coast and Florida. A bird that prefers to nest near water in an open habitat. A colony nester, males do not participate in nest building, incubation or raising of young. Males rarely fight, but females will squabble over nest sites and materials. Several females mate with one male. They are expanding northward, moving into northern states. Western populations tend to be larger than the eastern. Song varies from population to population.

AMERICAN CROW
Corvus brachyrhynchos

YEAR-ROUND
WINTER

Size: 18" (45 cm)

Male: All-black bird with black bill, legs and feet. Can have a purple sheen in direct sunlight.

Female: same as male

Juvenile: same as adult

Nest: platform; female builds; 1 brood per year

Eggs: 4-6; bluish to olive green, brown markings

Incubation: 18 days; female incubates

Fledging: 28-35 days; female and male feed young

Migration: non-migrator to partial migrator

Food: fruit, insects, mammals, fish, carrion; will come to seed and suet feeders

Compare: Similar to the Common Raven (pg. 29), but Crow has a smaller bill, lacks shaggy throat feathers and has a higher-pitched call than Raven's deep, low raspy call. The Crow has a squared tail. Raven has a wedge-shaped tail, apparent in flight. Black-billed Magpie (pg. 69) has a long tail and white belly.

Stan's Notes: One of the most recognizable birds in the state. Often reuses its nest every year if not taken over by a Great Horned Owl. Collects and stores bright, shiny objects in the nest. Able to mimic other birds and human voices. One of the smartest of all birds and very social, often entertaining itself by provoking chases with other birds. Feeds on road kill but is rarely hit by cars. Can live up to 20 years. Unmated birds known as helpers help raise the young. Large extended families roost together at night, dispersing during the day to hunt.

COMMON RAVEN
Corvus corax

Size: 22-27" (56-69 cm)

Male: Large all-black bird with a large black bill, a shaggy beard of feathers on the chin and throat, and a large wedge-shaped tail, seen in flight.

Female: same as male

Juvenile: same as adult

Nest: platform; female and male build; 1 brood per year

Eggs: 4-6; pale green with brown markings

Incubation: 18-21 days; female incubates

Fledging: 38-44 days; female and male feed young

Migration: non-migrator in California

Food: insects, fruit, small animals, carrion

Compare: Larger than its cousin, the American Crow (pg. 27), which lacks the throat patch of feathers. Glides on flat, outstretched wings unlike the slightly V-shaped pattern of the Crow. Low, raspy call distinguishes Raven from the higher-pitched Crow.

Stan's Notes: Considered by some to be the smartest of all birds. Known for its aerial acrobatics and long swooping dives. Scavenges with crows and gulls. Known to follow wolf packs around to pick up scraps and pick at bones of a kill. Complex courtship includes grabbing bills, preening each other and cooing. Most begin to breed at 3-4 years. Mates for life. Uses same nest site for many years.

soaring

DOUBLE-CRESTED CORMORANT
Phalacrocorax auritus

YEAR-ROUND
MIGRATION
SUMMER
WINTER

Size: 33" (84 cm)

Male: Large all-black water bird with long snake-like neck. A long yellow orange bill with a hooked tip.

Female: same as male

Juvenile: lighter brown with a grayish chest and neck

Nest: platform, in colony; male and female build; 1 brood per year

Eggs: 3-4; bluish white without markings

Incubation: 25-29 days; female and male incubate

Fledging: 37-42 days; male and female feed young

Migration: non-migrator to partial in California

Food: small fish, aquatic insects

Compare: Similar size as the Turkey Vulture (pg. 31), which also perches on branches with wings open to dry in sun, but Vulture has a naked red head. Twice the size of American Coot (pg. 21), which lacks the Cormorant's long neck and long pointed bill.

Stan's Notes: Often seen flying in large V formation. Often roosts in large groups in trees near water. Catches fish by swimming with wings held at its sides. To dry off it strikes an erect pose with wings outstretched, facing the sun. The name refers to its nearly invisible crests. "Cormorant" comes from the Latin *corvus*, meaning "crow," and *L. marinus*, meaning "pertaining to the sea," literally, "Sea Crow."

BLACK PHOEBE
Sayornis nigricans

Size: 7" (18 cm)

Male: A black head, neck, breast and back with a white belly and undertail. Long narrow tail. Dark eyes, bill and legs. Can raise and lower its small crest.

Female: same as male

Juvenile: similar to adult, brown-to-tan wing bars

Nest: cup; female builds; 1-2 broods per year

Eggs: 3-6; white without markings

Incubation: 15-17 days; female incubates

Fledging: 14-21 days; female and male feed young

Migration: partial to non-migrator; moves around after breeding to find food

Food: insects

Compare: Distinctive black and white pattern makes identification easy. Watch for tail to pump up and down very quickly when perched. The male Vermilion Flycatcher (pg. 357) is crimson and black. Say's Phoebe (pg. 271) has a pale orange belly and gray head.

Stan's Notes: Often seen in shrubby areas near water. Feeds mostly on insects near the surface of water. In the winter it feeds on insects near the ground. Like other flycatchers, perches on thin branches, flies out to snatch a passing insect and returns to perch. Pumps or bobs tail up and down quickly while perching. Male performs an aerial song and flight with a slow descent to attract a mate. Female builds shallow nest of mud, adhered to rocks or bridges, lined with hair and grass. Often uses same nest or location for several years.

RED-BREASTED SAPSUCKER
Sphyrapicus ruber

YEAR-ROUND
MIGRATION
SUMMER
WINTER

Size: 8½" (22 cm)

Male: Black and white body, wings and tail. Belly is white to pale yellow. Red head, chest and nape. White mark over bill.

Female: similar to male

Juvenile: similar to adult, lacking any red

Nest: cavity; female and male build; 1-2 broods per year

Eggs: 3-7; white without markings

Incubation: 12-14 days; female and male incubate

Fledging: 25-29 days; female and male feed young

Migration: partial to non-migrator in California

Food: insects, tree sap, berries

Compare: Male Williamson's Sapsucker (pg. 47) lacks the red head and has a bright yellow belly.

Stan's Notes: The most common sapsucker species in California. Most common in higher elevations. Rare in residential areas or city parks. An important species because nests are subsequently used by many cavity-nesting bird species, such as Mountain Bluebirds, that don't excavate their own. Excavates a nest cavity in a dead or dying deciduous tree such as cottonwood, aspen, birch or willow. Drills a horizontal grid pattern of holes from which it drinks sap and eats insects attracted to the sap. Will also eat berries.

male

female

HAIRY WOODPECKER
Picoides villosus

YEAR-ROUND

Size: 9" (22.5 cm)

Male: Black-and-white woodpecker with a white belly, and black wings with rows of white spots. White stripe down back. Long black bill. Red mark on back of head.

Female: same as male, but lacks a red mark on head

Juvenile: grayer version of female

Nest: cavity; female and male excavate; 1 brood per year

Eggs: 3-6; white without markings

Incubation: 11-15 days; female and male incubate, the female during day, male at night

Fledging: 28-30 days; male and female feed young

Migration: non-migrator

Food: insects, nuts, seeds; comes to seed and suet feeders

Compare: Larger than Downy Woodpecker (pg. 35) and has a longer bill. Nuttall's Woodpecker (pg. 39) lacks a large white stripe on back.

Stan's Notes: A common woodpecker of wooded backyards that announces its arrival with a sharp chirp before landing on feeders. This bird is responsible for eating many destructive forest insects. Has a barbed tongue, which helps it extract insects from trees. Tiny bristle-like feathers at the base of bill protect the nostrils from wood dust. Drums on hollow logs, branches or stovepipes in springtime to announce its territory. Often prefers to excavate nest cavities in live aspen trees. Has a larger, more oval-shaped cavity entrance than that of Downy Woodpecker.

male

female

ACORN WOODPECKER
Melanerpes formicivorus

YEAR-ROUND

Size: 9" (22.5 cm)

Male: A black and white woodpecker with an all-black back and prominent white eyes. Red cap and nape of neck. White forehead and cheeks. White rump and tips of wings, seen in flight.

Female: same as male, but has a smaller bill and less red on head

Juvenile: similar to adult of the same sex

Nest: cavity; male and female excavate; 1 brood per year

Eggs: 3-7; white without markings

Incubation: 11-12 days; female and male incubate

Fledging: 30-32 days; female and male feed young

Migration: non-migrator

Food: nuts, fruit, insects, sap; comes to suet and seed feeders

Compare: Lewis's Woodpecker (pg. 331) is larger and lacks the white on head and the red cap.

Stan's Notes: A woodpecker that depends upon acorns and other nuts for survival. Dead trees are very important to this species, as they are to all woodpeckers. Drills uniform holes in trees and telephone poles, where it wedges acorns and other nuts, storing them for later consumption. Unlike other woodpeckers, it lives and nests in small colonies. Colonies consist of up to 5 males, 1-2 females and up to 12 juveniles from previous years. All members help to raise the new young. This is a very vocal species, giving a loud, nasal, "wheka-wheka-wheka" call.

female

male

WILLIAMSON'S SAPSUCKER
Sphyrapicus thyroideus

YEAR-ROUND

Size: 9" (22.5 cm)

Male: More black than white with a red chin and bright yellow belly. Bold white stripes just above and below the eyes. White rump and wing patches flash when in flight.

Female: finely barred black-and-white back with a brown head, yellow belly, no wing patches

Juvenile: similar to female

Nest: cavity; male excavates; 1 brood per year

Eggs: 3-7; pale white without markings

Incubation: 12-14 days; male and female incubate

Fledging: 21-28 days; female and male feed young

Migration: non-migrator in California

Food: insects, tree sap

Compare: Lewis's Woodpecker (pg. 331) has a red face and belly. Female Williamson's is similar to the Northern Flicker (pg. 167), but Flicker has a gray head and brown and black back.

Stan's Notes: Largest sapsucker species with a striking difference between the male and female. Male drums early in spring to attract a mate and claim territory. Like the drumming of other sapsuckers, Williamson's drumming has an irregular cadence. Male excavates a new cavity each year, frequently in the same tree. Male does more incubating than the female. Occupies coniferous forests, foraging for insects and drilling uniform rows of holes from which tree sap oozes. Feeds upon the sap and insects that are attracted to the sap. Warblers and other bird species also feed from these taps. Sap wells are nearly exclusively in conifers.

winter

breeding

RUDDY TURNSTONE
Arenaria interpres

WINTER

Size: 9½" (24 cm)

Male: Breeding has orange legs, a black and white head marking, black bib, white breast and belly, black and chestnut wings and back. Slightly upturned black bill. Winter has a brown and white head and breast pattern.

Female: similar to male, only duller

Juvenile: similar to adults, but black and white head has a scaly appearance

Nest: ground; female builds; 1 brood per year

Eggs: 3-4; olive green with dark markings

Incubation: 22-24 days; male and female incubate

Fledging: 19-21 days; male feeds young

Migration: complete, to the California coast and South America

Food: aquatic insects, fish, mollusks, crustaceans, worms, eggs

Compare: Unusually ornamented shorebird. Look for a striking black and white pattern on head and neck, and orange legs to identify.

Stan's Notes: Winters along the coast. Also known as Rock Plover. Named "Turnstone" because it turns stones over on rocky beaches to find food. Known for its unusual behavior of robbing and eating other birds' eggs. Hangs around crabbing operations to eat scraps from nets. Can be very tolerant of humans when feeding. Females often leave before their young leave the nests (fledge), resulting in males raising the young. Males have a bare spot on the belly (brood patch) to warm the young, something only females normally have.

winter pg. 295

breeding

BLACK-BELLIED PLOVER
Pluvialis squatarola

WINTER

Size:	11-12" (28-30 cm)
Male:	Striking black and white breeding plumage. A black belly, chest, sides, face and neck. White cap, nape of neck and belly near tail. Black legs and bill.
Female:	less black on belly and chest than male
Juvenile:	grayer than adults, with much less black
Nest:	ground; male and female construct; 1 brood per year
Eggs:	3-4; pinkish or greenish with black-brown markings
Incubation:	26-27 days; male and female incubate, the male during day, female at night
Fledging:	35-45 days; male feeds young, young learn quickly to feed themselves
Migration:	complete, to coastal California, Mexico and Central and South America
Food:	insects
Compare:	The Snowy Plover (pg. 361) is smaller and lacks a black belly, chest and face.

Stan's Notes: Males perform a "butterfly" courtship flight to attract females. Female leaves male and young about 12 days after the eggs hatch. Breeds at age 3. Arrivals begin in July and August (autumn migration). Leaves in April. Doesn't breed in California. In flight, in any plumage, displays a white rump and stripe on wings with black axillaries (armpits). Often darts over ground to grab a bug and run.

female pg. 177

male

BUFFLEHEAD
Bucephala albeola

YEAR-ROUND
WINTER

Size: 13-15" (33-38 cm)

Male: A small duck with striking white sides and black back. Green purple head with a large white bonnet-like patch.

Female: brown version of male, with a brown head and white patch on cheek, just behind eyes

Juvenile: similar to female

Nest: cavity; female lines old woodpecker cavity; 1 brood per year

Eggs: 8-10; ivory to olive without markings

Incubation: 29-31 days; female incubates

Fledging: 50-55 days; female leads young to food

Migration: complete, to California, Mexico and Central America

Food: aquatic insects

Compare: The male Common Goldeneye (pg. 67) is slightly larger, shares the white sides and black back, but lacks the white head patch. Male Hooded Merganser (pg. 63) is similar, but lacks the male Bufflehead's white sides.

Stan's Notes: Common diving duck that travels with other ducks. Seen during migration and throughout winter, arriving in the state late in August. Found on rivers and lakes. Nests in old woodpecker cavities. Unlike other ducks, young stay in nests for up to two days before venturing out with their mothers. Female is very territorial and remains with the same mate for many years.

BLACK-NECKED STILT
Himantopus mexicanus

Size: 14" (36 cm)

Male: Upper parts of the head, neck and back are black. Lower parts are white. Ridiculously long red-to-pink legs. Long black bill.

Female: similar to male, only browner on back

Juvenile: similar to female, brown instead of black

Nest: ground; female and male construct; 1 brood per year

Eggs: 3-5; off-white with dark markings

Incubation: 22-26 days; female and male incubate, the male during day, female at night

Fledging: 28-32 days; female and male feed young

Migration: non-migrator to partial in California

Food: aquatic insects

Compare: Outrageous length of the red-to-pink legs make this shorebird hard to confuse with any other.

Stan's Notes: Seen year-round along the coast and as far north as the Great Lakes. This is a very vocal bird of shallow freshwater and saltwater marshes, giving a "kek-kek-kek" call. Legs are up to 10 inches (25 cm) long and may be the longest legs in the bird world in proportion to the body. It nests solitarily or in small colonies in open areas. Known for transporting water with water-soaked belly feathers (belly-soaking) to cool eggs during hot weather. This bird aggressively defends its nest, eggs and young. Young leave the nest shortly after hatching.

YELLOW-BILLED MAGPIE
Pica nutalli

YEAR-ROUND

Size: 16½" (41.5 cm)

Male: A black head, neck and upper breast and back. White lower breast and belly. Wings and tail appear black but are an iridescent blue to green. Distinctive yellow bill.

Female: same as male

Juvenile: similar to adult

Nest: modified cup; female and male construct; 1 brood per year

Eggs: 4-7; olive with brown markings

Incubation: 16-18 days; female incubates

Fledging: 30-35 days; female and male feed young

Migration: non-migrator

Food: insects, fruit, carrion (road kill), seeds

Compare: Black-billed Magpie (pg. 69) is larger and has a black bill and slightly longer tail.

Stan's Notes: A species found only in California (endemic). Very similar to the Black-billed Magpie in voice and appearance. Spends a lot of time on the ground. Walks and hops in search of insects or seeds. Three-quarters of diet is insects. Known to cache acorns and other foodstuffs in trees, presumably for later consumption. Slow, steady wing beats in flight, similar to the pattern of rowing a boat. Mated pairs raise wings, bow to each other and male feeds female. This behavior is believed to strengthen the pair bond. Male feeds female while she incubates. Pairs stay together throughout the year. Can be long-term mates. Usually is seen with other Yellow-billeds, often family members. Nests in small colonies. Large domed nest is built high up, usually in a dense stand of trees.

female pg. 193

male

LESSER SCAUP
Aythya affinis

YEAR-ROUND
MIGRATION
WINTER

Size: 16-17" (40-43 cm)

Male: Appears mostly black with bold white sides and gray back. Chest and head look nearly black, but head appears purple with green highlights in direct sun. Bright yellow eyes.

Female: overall brown with dull white patch at base of light gray bill, yellow eyes

Juvenile: same as female

Nest: ground; female builds; 1 brood per year

Eggs: 8-14; olive buff without markings

Incubation: 22-28 days; female incubates

Fledging: 45-50 days; female teaches young to feed

Migration: complete, to California, Mexico, Central America and northern South America

Food: aquatic plants and insects

Compare: The male Ring-necked Duck (pg. 61) has a bold white ring around its bill, a black back and lacks the bold white sides of the male Lesser Scaup. The male Blue-winged Teal (pg. 189) is slightly smaller and has a bright white crescent-shaped mark at base of bill.

Stan's Notes: A common diving duck. Often seen in large flocks on lakes, ponds and sewage lagoons. Completely submerges itself to feed on the bottom of lakes (unlike dabbling ducks, which only tip forward to reach the bottom). Note the bold white stripe under the wings when in flight. Has an interesting baby-sitting arrangement in which groups of young are tended by 1-3 adult females. A winter resident. Doesn't breed in most of California.

female pg. 197

male

RING-NECKED DUCK
Aythya collaris

Size: 17" (43 cm)

Male: A striking duck with black head, chest and back. Sides are gray to nearly white. A light blue bill with a bold white ring and second ring at base of bill. Top of head is peaked.

Female: dark brown back, light brown sides, a gray face, dark brown crown, white line behind eyes, white ring around a light blue bill, top of head is peaked

Juvenile: similar to female

Nest: ground; female builds; 1 brood per year

Eggs: 8-10; olive gray to brown without markings

Incubation: 26-27 days; female incubates

Fledging: 49-56 days; female teaches young to feed

Migration: complete, to California, Mexico and Central America

Food: aquatic plants and insects

Compare: Similar size as male Lesser Scaup (pg. 59), which has a gray back unlike the black back of male Ring-necked Duck. Look for male Ring-necked's bold white ring around bill.

Stan's Notes: Common winter duck throughout the state. A diving duck, watch for it to dive underwater to forage for food. Takes to flight by springing up off water. Was named "Ring-necked" because of the cinnamon collar (nearly impossible to see in the field). Also called Ring-billed Duck due to the white ring on its bill.

female pg. 199

male

HOODED MERGANSER
Lophodytes cucullatus

WINTER

Size: 16-19" (40-48 cm)

Male: A sleek black-and-white bird that has rusty brown sides. Crest "hood" raises to reveal a large white patch on the head. Long, thin black bill.

Female: sleek brown and rust bird with a ragged rusty crest and long, thin brown bill

Juvenile: similar to female

Nest: cavity; female lines old woodpecker hole; 1 brood per year

Eggs: 10-12; white without markings

Incubation: 32-33 days; female incubates

Fledging: 71 days; female feeds young

Migration: complete, to northwestern California

Food: small fish, aquatic insects

Compare: A distinctive diving bird, look for the male's large white patch "hood" on the head and rusty brown sides. Male Bufflehead (pg. 53) is smaller than Hooded Merganser and has white sides. The male Wood Duck (pg. 333) is similar in size, but has a green head.

Stan's Notes: A small diving bird of shallow-water ponds, sloughs, lakes and rivers. Male Hooded Merganser can voluntarily raise and lower its crest to show off the large white head patch. Rarely found away from wooded areas, where it nests in natural cavities or nest boxes. The female will "dump" her eggs into other female Hooded Merganser nests, resulting in 20-25 eggs in some nests. Known to share a nest cavity with a Wood Duck, sitting side by side.

winter

breeding

AMERICAN AVOCET
Recurvirostra americana

Size: 18" (45 cm)

Male: Black and white back, white belly. A long, thin upturned bill and long gray legs. Head and neck rusty red during breeding, gray in the winter.

Female: similar to male, only with a more strongly upturned bill

Juvenile: similar to adults, with a slight wash of rusty red on neck and head

Nest: ground; female and male construct; 1 brood per year

Eggs: 3-5; light olive with brown markings

Incubation: 22-29 days; female and male incubate

Fledging: 28-35 days; female and male feed young

Migration: non-migrator to partial in California

Food: insects, crustaceans, aquatic plants, fruit

Compare: The Oystercatcher (pg. 23) is the same size with shorter yellow legs and a large reddish orange bill. Ibis (pg. 227) is larger and has a down-curved bill. Look for the rusty red head of breeding Avocet and upturned bill.

Stan's Notes: A handsome long-legged bird that prefers shallow alkaline, saline or brackish water, it is well adapted to arid western U.S. conditions. Uses its up-curved bill to sweep from side to side across mud bottoms in search of insects. Both the male and female have a brood patch to incubate eggs and brood their young. Nests in loose colonies of up to 20 pairs. All members of the colony will defend together against intruders.

male

female pg. 209

COMMON GOLDENEYE
Bucephala clangula

WINTER

Size: 18½-20" (47-50 cm)

Male: A mostly white duck with a black back and large, puffy green head. Large white spot in front of each bright golden eye. Dark bill.

Female: brown and gray, a large dark brown head, gray body, white collar, bright golden eyes, yellow-tipped dark bill

Juvenile: same as female, but has a dark bill

Nest: cavity; female lines old woodpecker cavity; 1 brood per year

Eggs: 8-10; light green without markings

Incubation: 28-32 days; female incubates

Fledging: 56-59 days; female leads young to food

Migration: complete, to California and Mexico

Food: aquatic plants, insects

Compare: Similar to, but larger than, the black and white male Lesser Scaup (pg. 59). Look for the distinctive white mark in front of each golden eye, and a white breast. Larger than the breeding male Ruddy Duck (pg. 185), which lacks the green head.

Stan's Notes: Known for its loud whistling, produced by its wings in flight. In late winter and early spring, male often attracts female through elaborate displays, throwing its head backward while it utters a single raspy note. Female will lay eggs in other goldeneye nests, which results in some mothers incubating up to 30 eggs. Received the common name from its obvious bright golden eyes. Winters in California where it finds open water.

YEAR-ROUND

BLACK-BILLED MAGPIE
Pica hudsonia

Size: 20" (50 cm)

Male: A large black-and-white bird with very long tail and white belly. Iridescent green wings and tail in direct sunlight. Large black bill and legs. White wing patches flash in flight.

Female: same as male

Juvenile: same as adult, but shorter tail

Nest: modified pendulous; the female and male build; 1 brood per year

Eggs: 5-8; green with brown markings

Incubation: 16-21 days; female incubates

Fledging: 25-29 days; female and male feed young

Migration: non-migrator

Food: insects, carrion, fruit, seeds

Compare: The Yellow-billed Magpie (pg. 57) is smaller and has a yellow bill. Larger than the Great-tailed Grackle (pg. 25). Contrasting colors and very long tail of Magpie differentiate it from the all-black American Crow (pg. 27).

Stan's Notes: A wonderfully intelligent bird that is able to mimic dogs, cats and even people. Will often raid a barnyard dog dish for food. Feeds on a variety of food from road kill to insects and seeds it collects from the ground. Easily identified by its bold black-and-white colors and long streaming tail. Travels in small flocks, usually family members, and tends to be very gregarious. Breeds in small colonies. Unusual dome nest (dome-shaped roof) deep within thick shrubs. Mates with same mate for several years. Prefers open fields with cattle or sheep, where it feeds on insects attracted to livestock.

BLACK-CROWNED NIGHT-HERON
Nycticorax nycticorax

YEAR-ROUND
SUMMER

Size: 22-27" (56-69 cm)

Male: A stocky, hunched and inactive heron with black back and crown, white belly and gray wings. Long dark bill, short yellow legs and bright red eyes. Breeding adult has 2 long white plumes on crown.

Female: same as male

Juvenile: golden brown head and back with white spots, streaked breast, yellow orange eyes, brown bill

Nest: platform; female and male build; 1 brood per year

Eggs: 3-5; light blue without markings

Incubation: 24-26 days; female and male incubate

Fledging: 42-48 days; female and male feed young

Migration: non-migrator to partial in California

Food: fish, aquatic insects

Compare: Half the size of Great Blue Heron (pg. 319) when perching. Look for a short-necked heron with a black back and crown.

Stan's Notes: A very secretive bird, this heron is most active near dawn and dusk (crepuscular). It hunts alone, but nests in small colonies. Roosts in trees during the day. Often squawks if disturbed from the daytime roost. Often seen being harassed by other herons during days.

rushing

weed dance

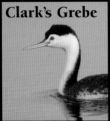

Clark's Grebe

WESTERN GREBE
Aechmophorus occidentalis

Size: 24" (60 cm)

Male: A long-necked, nearly all-black water bird with white chin, neck, chest and belly. Long greenish yellow bill. Bright red eyes. Dark crown extends around eyes to base of bill. In winter, becomes light gray around eyes.

Female: same as male

Juvenile: similar to adult

Nest: platform; female and male build; 1 brood per year

Eggs: 3-4; bluish white with brown markings

Incubation: 20-23 days; female and male incubate

Fledging: 65-75 days; female and male feed young

Migration: non-migrator to partial in California

Food: fish, aquatic insects

Compare: Striking black and white plumage makes it hard to confuse with any other bird.

Stan's Notes: Well known for its unusual breeding dance known as rushing. Side by side, with necks outstretched, mates spring to their webbed feet and dance across the water's surface, diving underwater at the end of the rush. Often holds long stalks of water plants in bill when courting (weed dance). Legs are far back on the body, making it hard to walk on the ground. Shortly after choosing a large lake for breeding and till late in summer, it rarely flies. Young ride on backs of adults, climbing on minutes after hatching. Nests in large colonies of up to 100 pairs on lakes with tall vegetation. Nearly identical to Clark's Grebe (see inset), which has a bright yellow bill and white on the neck and face extending above the eyes.

soaring

juvenile

BALD EAGLE
Haliaeetus leucocephalus

Size: 31-37" (79-94 cm); up to 7-foot wingspan

Male: Pure white head and tail contrast with dark brown-to-black body and wings. A large, curved yellow bill and yellow feet.

Female: same as male, only slightly larger

Juvenile: dark brown with white spots or speckles throughout body and wings, gray bill

Nest: massive platform, usually in a tree; female and male build; 1 brood per year

Eggs: 2; off-white without markings

Incubation: 34-36 days; female and male incubate

Fledging: 75-90 days; female and male feed young

Migration: partial to complete, to California

Food: fish, carrion, birds (mainly ducks)

Compare: Golden Eagle (pg. 235) and Turkey Vulture (pg. 31) lack the white head and white tail of adult Bald Eagle. Juvenile Golden Eagle, with its white wrist marks and white base of tail, is similar to the juvenile Bald Eagle.

Stan's Notes: Driven to near extinction due to DDT poisoning and illegal killing. Now making a comeback in North America. Returns to same nest each year, adding more sticks, enlarging it to massive proportions, at times up to 1,000 pounds (450 kg). In the midair mating ritual, one eagle will flip upside down and lock talons with another. Both tumble, then break apart to continue flight. Thought to mate for life, but will switch mates if not successful reproducing. Juvenile attains the white head and tail at about 4-5 years of age. A winter resident except for a few scattered locations.

soaring

juvenile

CALIFORNIA CONDOR
Gymnogyps californianus

Size: 44-46" (112-117 cm); up to 9½-ft. wingspan

Male: Black with splayed "fingertips" on wings and white wing linings, as seen in flight. Ruffle of feathers around neck. Orange-to-red head. Small dark patch between eyes. Short tail.

Female: same as male

Juvenile: similar to adult, but gray head and lacks the white wing linings

Nest: no nest; lays egg on a coarse gravel bed on cave floor; 0-1 brood per year

Eggs: 1; pale green without markings

Incubation: 42-50 days; female and male incubate

Fledging: 160-180 days; female and male feed young

Migration: non-migrator to partial; moves to find food

Food: carrion

Compare: Turkey Vulture (pg. 31) is smaller with gray trailing edges of wings. The Golden Eagle (pg. 235) is smaller and has a white base of tail. Most California Condors in the wild are marked with numbered, colored wing tags.

Stan's Notes: One of the largest flying birds in North America. Can soar to 15,000 feet (4,575 m). A vulture, mistaken for small aircraft. Slow wing beats. Nearly extinct in the 1980s. Populations unstable. Usually silent, will hiss if approached at nest. Matures at 6-7 years. Long-term pair bond. Most breed every other year. Presumed to live 40 years, perhaps up to 70. May be more closely related to storks. Feet are weaker than feet of eagles or hawks.

BLUE-GRAY GNATCATCHER
Polioptila caerulea

YEAR-ROUND
SUMMER

Size: 4" (10 cm)

Male: A light blue-to-gray head, back, breast and wings, with a black forehead and eyebrows. White belly and prominent white eye-ring. Long black tail with a white undertail, often held cocked above the rest of body.

Female: same as male, only grayer and lacking black on head

Juvenile: similar to female

Nest: cup; female and male build; 1 brood a year

Eggs: 4-5; pale blue with dark markings

Incubation: 10-13 days; female and male incubate

Fledging: 10-12 days; female and male feed young

Migration: complete, to southern California, Mexico, Central America

Food: insects

Compare: The breeding male California Gnatcatcher (pg. 247) has a black cap. Very active near the nest, look for it flitting around upper branches in search of insects.

Stan's Notes: Found in a wide variety of scrublands in California. Listen for its wheezy call notes to help locate. A fun and easy bird to watch. Flicks its tail up and down and from side to side while calling. Common cowbird host. Returns to California by mid-April, with most leaving by late August. Although population is abundant and widespread, it has been decreasing in the recent past.

female pg. 113

male

LAZULI BUNTING
Passerina amoena

Size: 5½" (14 cm)

Male: A turquoise blue head, neck, back and tail. Cinnamon chest with cinnamon extending down flanks slightly. White belly. Two bold white wing bars. Non-breeding male has a spotty blue head and back.

Female: overall grayish brown, warm brown breast, a light wash of blue on wings and tail, gray throat, light gray belly and 2 narrow white wing bars

Juvenile: similar to adult of the same sex

Nest: cup; female builds; 2-3 broods per year

Eggs: 3-5; pale blue without markings

Incubation: 11-13 days; female incubates

Fledging: 10-12 days; female and male feed young

Migration: complete, to Mexico

Food: insects, seeds

Compare: The male Western Bluebird (pg. 91) is larger and darker blue with a darker brown breast. Male Blue Grosbeak (pg. 87) has chestnut wing bars and lacks a white belly.

Stan's Notes: More common in shrub lands in California. Doesn't like dense forests. Strong association with water such as rivers and streams. Gathers in small flocks and tends to move up in elevations after breeding to hunt for insects and look for seeds. Has increased in population and expanded its range over the last century.

TREE SWALLOW
Tachycineta bicolor

YEAR-ROUND
MIGRATION
SUMMER
WINTER

Size: 5-6" (13-15 cm)

Male: Blue green in the spring and greener in fall. Appears to change color in direct sunlight. A white belly, a notched tail and pointed wing tips.

Female: similar to male, only duller

Juvenile: gray brown with a white belly and grayish breast band

Nest: cavity; female and male line former woodpecker cavity or nest box; 1 brood per year

Eggs: 4-6; white without markings

Incubation: 13-16 days; female incubates

Fledging: 20-24 days; female and male feed young

Migration: complete, to Mexico and Central America

Food: insects

Compare: The Barn Swallow (pg. 85) has a rust belly and deeply forked tail. Similar size as the Cliff Swallow (pg. 115), but lacks any tan-to-rust coloring.

Stan's Notes: The first swallow species to return in spring. Many stay year-round or migrate only as far south as southern California. Can be seen throughout the state, but most common along coastal beaches, freshwater ponds, lakes and agricultural fields. Attracted to your yard with a nest box. Competes with Western and Mountain Bluebirds for cavities or nest boxes. Will travel great distances to find dropped feathers to line its grass nest. Sometimes seen playing, chasing after dropped feathers. Often seen flying back and forth across fields, feeding on insects. Gathers in large flocks to migrate.

BARN SWALLOW
Hirundo rustica

Size: 7" (18 cm)

Male: A sleek swallow with a blue black back, a cinnamon belly and a reddish brown chin. White spots on long forked tail.

Female: same as male, only slightly duller

Juvenile: similar to adults, with a tan belly and chin, and shorter tail

Nest: cup; female and male build; 2 broods a year

Eggs: 4-5; white with brown markings

Incubation: 13-17 days; female incubates

Fledging: 18-23 days; female and male feed young

Migration: complete, to South America

Food: insects, prefers beetles, wasps and flies

Compare: Tree Swallow (pg. 83) has a white belly and chin and a notched tail. The Cliff Swallow (pg. 115) is smaller and lacks a distinctive, deeply forked tail.

Stan's Notes: Of the seven swallow species in California, this is the only one with a deeply forked tail. Unlike other swallows, Barn Swallow rarely glides in flight, so look for continuous flapping. It builds a mud nest using up to 1,000 beak-loads of mud, often in or on barns. Nests in colonies of 4-6 individuals, but nesting alone isn't uncommon. Drinks in flight, skimming water or getting water from wet leaves. Also bathes while flying through rain or sprinklers.

female
pg. 131

male

BLUE GROSBEAK
Passerina caerulea

MIGRATION
SUMMER

Size: 7" (18 cm)

Male: Overall blue bird with 2 chestnut wing bars. Large gray-to-silver bill. Black around base of bill.

Female: overall brown with darker wings and tail, 2 tan wing bars, large gray-to-silver bill

Juvenile: similar to female

Nest: cup; female builds; 1-2 broods per year

Eggs: 3-6; pale blue without markings

Incubation: 11-12 days; female incubates

Fledging: 9-10 days; female and male feed young

Migration: complete, to Mexico and Central America

Food: insects, seeds; will come to seed feeders

Compare: The male Lazuli Bunting (pg. 81) has 2 bold white wing bars and a white belly. The male Mountain and Western Bluebirds (pp. 89 and 91, respectively) are the same size, but lack the male Grosbeak's chestnut wing bars and oversized bill.

Stan's Notes: This bird returns to California by early May. It has expanded northward with overall populations increasing over the past 30-40 years. A bird of semi-open habitats such as overgrown fields, riversides, woodland edges and fencerows. Frequently seen twitching and spreading its tail. First-year males show only some blue, obtaining the full complement of blue feathers in the second winter. Visits seed feeders.

male

female

MOUNTAIN BLUEBIRD
Sialia currucoides

SUMMER
WINTER

Size: 7" (18 cm)

Male: An overall sky blue bird with a darker blue head, back, wings and tail and white lower belly. Thin black bill.

Female: similar to male, but paler with a nearly gray head and chest and a whitish belly

Juvenile: similar to adult of the same sex

Nest: cavity, old woodpecker cavity, wooden nest box; female builds; 1-2 broods per year

Eggs: 4-6; pale blue without markings

Incubation: 13-14 days; female incubates

Fledging: 22-23 days; female and male feed young

Migration: complete, to parts of California, Mexico

Food: insects

Compare: Similar to Western Bluebird (pg. 91), but not as dark blue and lacks Western's rusty red chest. Same size as male Blue Grosbeak (pg. 87), but lacks the Grosbeak's chestnut wing bars and oversized bill.

Stan's Notes: This bird is common in open mountainous country. Due to conservation of suitable nest sites (dead trees with cavities and man-made nest boxes), populations increased over the past 30 years. Like other bluebirds, Mountain Bluebirds take well to nest boxes and tolerate close contact with humans. Young will imprint on their first nest box or cavity, then choose a similar type of box or cavity throughout the rest of life.

male

female

WESTERN BLUEBIRD
Sialia mexicana

YEAR-ROUND WINTER

Size: 7" (18 cm)

Male: Deep blue head, neck, back, wings and tail. Rusty red chest and flanks.

Female: similar to male, only duller with gray head

Juvenile: similar to female, with a speckled chest

Nest: cavity, old woodpecker cavity, wooden nest box; female builds; 1-2 broods per year

Eggs: 4-6; pale blue without markings

Incubation: 13-14 days; female incubates

Fledging: 22-23 days; female and male feed young

Migration: non-migrator to partial in California

Food: insects, fruit

Compare: Mountain Bluebird (pg. 89) is similar, but lacks the rusty red breast. Larger than male Lazuli Bunting (pg. 81), which has white wing bars. Same size as male Blue Grosbeak (pg. 87), but lacks the Grosbeak's chestnut wing bars and oversized bill.

Stan's Notes: More widespread than Mountain Bluebirds. Found in a variety of habitats, from agricultural land to clear-cuts. Requires a cavity for nesting. Competes with starlings for nest cavities. Like the Mountain Bluebird, it uses nest boxes, which are responsible for the stable populations. The courting male will fly in front of the female, spreading wings and tail, then perch next to her. Often seen going in and out of nest box or cavity as if to say, "Look inside." Male may offer food to female to establish pair bond.

STELLER'S JAY
Cyanocitta stelleri

YEAR-ROUND

Size: 11" (28 cm)

Male: Dark blue wings, tail and belly. Black head, nape and breast. Large, pointed black crest on head that can be lifted at will.

Female: same as male

Juvenile: similar to adult

Nest: cup; female and male build; 1 brood a year

Eggs: 3-5; pale green with brown markings

Incubation: 14-16 days; female incubates

Fledging: 16-18 days; female and male feed young

Migration: non-migrator

Food: insects, berries, seeds; will visit seed feeders

Compare: The Western Scrub-Jay (pg. 95) lacks the Steller's crest and all-black head.

Stan's Notes: Common resident of coniferous forests from sea level to timberline. Often found in suburban yards. Thought to mate for life, rarely dispersing far, usually breeding within 10 miles (16 km) of birthplace. Several subspecies found throughout the Southwest. The California form (shown) has a black crest and lacks any distinct white streaks on head. Usually very bold where it comes in contact with people on a regular basis such as a campground. Often seen in small flocks consisting mainly of family members. Feeds on a wide variety of food, but seeds make up 70 percent of the diet. Will cache seeds and acorns for later consumption. Was named after the Arctic explorer Georg W. Steller, who is said to have discovered the bird on the coast of Alaska in 1741.

Island Scrub-Jay

WESTERN SCRUB-JAY
Aphelocoma californica

YEAR-ROUND

Size: 11" (28 cm)

Male: Head, wings, tail and breast band are deep blue. Brownish patch on back. Chin, breast and belly are dull white. Very long tail.

Female: same as male

Juvenile: similar to adult, overall gray with light blue wings and tail

Nest: cup; female and male build; 1 brood a year

Eggs: 3-6; pale green with red brown markings

Incubation: 15-17 days; female incubates

Fledging: 18-20 days; female and male feed young

Migration: non-migrator

Food: insects, seeds, fruit; comes to seed feeders

Compare: Same size as Steller's Jay (pg. 93), but lacks the all-black head and pointed crest.

Stan's Notes: A tame bird of urban areas that visits feeders. Several subspecies occur with some regional variations in color, the Pacific race (shown) being the deepest blue. Island Scrub-Jay (see inset) is closely related, but found only on Santa Cruz Island. This species is darker blue and overall larger than the Western Scrub-Jay. Forms a long-term pair bond. The male feeds the female before and during incubation. Young of a pair remain close by for up to a couple years, helping parents raise subsequent siblings. Caches food by burying it for later consumption. Likely serves as a major distributor of oaks and pines by not returning to eat the seeds it buried.

male

female

BELTED KINGFISHER
Ceryle alcyon

YEAR-ROUND WINTER

Size: 13" (33 cm)

Male: Large blue bird with white belly. Broad blue gray breast band and a ragged crest that is raised and lowered at will. Large head with a long, thick black bill. A small white spot directly in front of red brown eyes. Black wing tips with splashes of white that flash when flying.

Female: same as male, but with rusty breast band in addition to blue gray band, and rusty flanks

Juvenile: similar to female

Nest: cavity; female and male excavate; 1 brood per year

Eggs: 6-7; white without markings

Incubation: 23-24 days; female and male incubate

Fledging: 23-24 days; female and male feed young

Migration: non-migrator to complete in California

Food: small fish

Compare: Larger than the Western Scrub-Jay (pg. 95). Kingfisher is rarely found away from water.

Stan's Notes: Seen perched on branches near the water, it dives headfirst for small fish and returns to a branch to eat. Has a loud machine-gun-like call. Excavates a deep cavity in bank of river or lake. Parents drop dead fish into water, teaching the young to dive. Regurgitates pellets of bone after meals, being unable to pass bones through digestive tract. Mates recognize each other by call.

CHESTNUT-BACKED CHICKADEE
Poecile rufescens

YEAR-ROUND

Size: 4¾" (12 cm)

Male: Rich, warm chestnut back and sides. Black crown and chin. White cheeks and sides of head. Gray wings and tail.

Female: same as male

Juvenile: same as adult

Nest: cavity; female and male build; 1-2 broods per year

Eggs: 5-7; white without markings

Incubation: 10-12 days; female incubates

Fledging: 13-16 days; female and male feed young

Migration: non-migrator

Food: insects, seeds, fruit; comes to seed and suet feeders

Compare: Mountain Chickadee (pg. 259) is similar, but lacks the Chestnut-backed's distinctive chestnut back.

Stan's Notes: The most colorful of all chickadees. Like the other chickadee species, the Chestnut-backed clings to branches upside down, looking for insects. During breeding, it is quiet and secretive. In winter it joins other birds such as kinglets, nuthatches and other chickadees. It prefers humid coniferous forests. Builds a cavity nest 2-20 feet (up to 6 m) above the ground. Will use the same nest year after year. Visits seed and suet feeders.

HOUSE WREN
Troglodytes aedon

YEAR-ROUND
MIGRATION
SUMMER
WINTER

Size: 5" (13 cm)

Male: A small all-brown bird with lighter brown markings on tail and wings. Slightly curved brown bill. Often holds its tail erect.

Female: same as male

Juvenile: same as adult

Nest: cavity; female and male line just about any nest cavity; 2 broods per year

Eggs: 4-6; tan with brown markings

Incubation: 10-13 days; female and male incubate

Fledging: 12-15 days; female and male feed young

Migration: complete, to California and Mexico, non-migrator in most of California

Food: insects

Compare: Bewick's Wren (pg. 117) is larger and has white eyebrows. Canyon Wren (pg. 147) is larger and has a white throat and breast.

Stan's Notes: A prolific songster, it will sing from dawn until dusk during the mating season. Easily attracted to nest boxes. In spring, the male chooses several prospective nesting cavities and places a few small twigs in each. Female inspects each, chooses one, and finishes the nest building. She will completely fill the nest cavity with uniformly small twigs, then line a small depression at back of cavity with pine needles and grass. Often has trouble fitting long twigs through nest cavity hole. Tries many different directions and approaches until successful.

PINE SISKIN
Carduelis pinus

Size: 5" (13 cm)

Male: Small brown finch. Heavily streaked back, breast and belly. Yellow wing bars. Yellow at base of tail. Thin bill.

Female: same as male

Juvenile: similar to adult, light yellow tinge over the breast and chin

Nest: modified cup; female constructs; 2 broods per year

Eggs: 3-4; greenish blue with brown markings

Incubation: 12-13 days; female incubates

Fledging: 14-15 days; female and male feed young

Migration: non-migrator to partial migrator; will move around the state in search of food

Food: seeds, insects; will come to seed feeders

Compare: Female American Goldfinch (pg. 387) lacks streaks and has white wing bars. Female House Finch (pg. 105) has a streaked chest, but lacks yellow wing bars.

Stan's Notes: A nesting resident, usually considered a winter finch. More visible in the non-nesting season, when it gathers in flocks, moves around California and visits feeders. Comes to thistle feeders. Travels and breeds in small groups. Male feeds the female during incubation. Juveniles lose yellow tint by late summer of the first year. Builds nest toward ends of coniferous branches, where needles are dense, helping to conceal. Nests are often only a few feet apart.

male pg. 355

female

YEAR-ROUND

HOUSE FINCH
Carpodacus mexicanus

Size: 5" (13 cm)

Female: A plain brown bird with a heavily streaked white chest.

Male: orange red face, chest and rump, a brown cap, brown marking behind eyes, brown wings streaked with white, streaked belly

Juvenile: similar to female

Nest: cup, sometimes in cavities; female builds; 2 broods per year

Eggs: 4-5; pale blue, lightly marked

Incubation: 12-14 days; female incubates

Fledging: 15-19 days; female and male feed young

Migration: non-migrator; moves around to find food

Food: seeds, fruit, leaf buds; will visit seed feeders

Compare: Similar to the Pine Siskin (pg. 103), but lacks the yellow wing bars and has a larger bill. Female American Goldfinch (pg. 387) has a clear chest and white wing bars.

Stan's Notes: Very social bird. Visits feeders in small flocks. Likes nesting in hanging flower baskets. Incubating female is fed by the male. Has a loud, cheerful warbling song. Historically it occurred from the Pacific coast to the Rockies, with only a few reaching the eastern side. House Finches that were originally introduced to Long Island, New York, from the western U.S. in the 1940s have since populated the entire eastern U.S. Now found all over the country. Can be the most common bird at your feeders. Suffers from a fatal eye disease that causes the eyes to crust over.

CHIPPING SPARROW
Spizella passerina

YEAR-ROUND
MIGRATION
SUMMER
WINTER

Size: 5" (13 cm)

Male: Small gray brown sparrow with a clear gray breast, rusty crown and white eyebrows. A black eye line and thin gray black bill. Two faint wing bars.

Female: same as male

Juvenile: similar to adult, has a streaked breast, lacks the rusty crown

Nest: cup; female builds; 2 broods per year

Eggs: 3-5; blue green with brown markings

Incubation: 11-14 days; female incubates

Fledging: 10-12 days; female and male feed young

Migration: complete to non-migrator in California

Food: insects, seeds; will come to ground feeders

Compare: Lark Sparrow (pg. 125) is larger and has a white chest and central spot. Song Sparrow (pg. 109) has a heavily streaked chest. Fox Sparrow (pg. 129) is larger and lacks the rusty crown. Female House Finch (pg. 105) has a streaked chest.

Stan's Notes: A common garden or yard bird, often seen feeding on dropped seeds beneath feeders. Gathers in large family groups to feed in preparation for migration. Migrates at night in flocks of 20-30 birds. The common name comes from the male's fast "chip" call. Often is just called Chippy. Nest is placed low in dense shrubs and is almost always lined with animal hair. Can be very unafraid of people, allowing you to approach closely before it flies away.

SONG SPARROW
Melospiza melodia

YEAR-ROUND

Size: 5-6" (13-15 cm)

Male: Common brown sparrow with heavy dark streaks on breast coalescing into a central dark spot.

Female: same as male

Juvenile: similar to adult, finely streaked breast, lacks a central spot

Nest: cup; female builds; 2 broods per year

Eggs: 3-4; pale blue to green with reddish brown markings

Incubation: 12-14 days; female incubates

Fledging: 9-12 days; female and male feed young

Migration: non-migrator in California

Food: insects, seeds; rarely visits seed feeders

Compare: Similar to other brown sparrows. Look for a heavily streaked chest with central dark spot.

Stan's Notes: Many Song Sparrow subspecies or varieties, but dark central spot carries through each variant. While the female builds another nest for a second brood, the male sparrow often takes over feeding the young. Returns to a similar area each year, defending a small territory by singing from thick shrubs. A common host of the Brown-headed Cowbird. Ground feeders, look for them to scratch simultaneously with both feet to expose seeds. Unlike many other sparrow species, Song Sparrows rarely flock together. A constant songster, repeating its loud, clear song every couple minutes. Song varies in structure, but is basically the same from region to region.

male pg. 257

female

Oregon female

DARK-EYED JUNCO
Junco hyemalis

YEAR-ROUND
WINTER

Size: 5½" (14 cm)

Female: A round, dark-eyed bird with tan-to-brown chest, head and back. White belly. Ivory-to-pink bill. Since the outermost tail feathers are white, tail appears as a white V in flight.

Male: same as female, only slate gray to charcoal

Juvenile: similar to female, but has a streaked breast and head

Nest: cup; female and male build; 2 broods a year

Eggs: 3-5; white with reddish brown markings

Incubation: 12-13 days; female incubates

Fledging: 10-13 days; male and female feed young

Migration: partial to non-migrator in California

Food: seeds, insects; will come to seed feeders

Compare: Rarely confused with any other bird. Small flocks feed under bird feeders in winter.

Stan's Notes: Several junco species have now been combined into one, simply called Dark-eyed Junco (see lower inset). It is one of the most numerous wintering birds in the state. A common year-round resident in parts of California. Spends the winter in the foothills and plains after snowmelt and returns to higher elevations to nest. Nests in a wide variety of wooded habitats during April and May. Adheres to a rigid social hierarchy, with the dominant birds chasing the less dominant birds. Look for its white outer tail feathers flashing when in flight. Most comfortable on the ground, juncos "double-scratch" with both feet to expose seeds and insects. Eats many weed seeds. Usually seen on the ground in small flocks.

male pg. 8

female

LAZULI BUNTING
Passerina amoena

MIGRATION
SUMMER

Size: 5½" (14 cm)

Female: Overall grayish brown with a warm brown chest, light wash of blue on wings and tail, gray throat and light gray belly. Two narrow white wing bars.

Male: turquoise blue head, neck, back and tail, cinnamon breast, white belly, 2 bold white wing bars

Juvenile: similar to adult of the same sex

Nest: cup; female builds; 2-3 broods per year

Eggs: 3-5; pale blue without markings

Incubation: 11-13 days; female incubates

Fledging: 10-12 days; female and male feed young

Migration: complete, to Mexico

Food: insects, seeds

Compare: Female Blue Grosbeak (pg. 131) is similar, but is overall darker and has tan wing bars. The female Western Bluebird (pg. 91) and Mountain Bluebird (pg. 89) are larger and have much more blue than female Bunting.

Stan's Notes: More common in shrub lands in California. Doesn't like dense forests. Strong association with water such as rivers and streams. Gathers in small flocks and tends to move up in elevations after breeding to hunt for insects and look for seeds. Has increased in population and expanded its range over the last century.

CLIFF SWALLOW
Petrochelidon pyrrhonota

Size: 5½" (14 cm)

Male: A uniquely patterned swallow with a dark back, wings and cap. Distinctive tan-to-rust rump, cheeks and forehead.

Female: same as male

Juvenile: similar to adult, lacks distinct patterning

Nest: gourd-shaped, made of mud; the male and female build; 1-2 broods per year

Eggs: 3-6; pale white with brown markings

Incubation: 14-16 days; male and female incubate

Fledging: 21-24 days; female and male feed young

Migration: complete, to South America

Food: insects

Compare: Smaller than Barn Swallow (pg. 85), which has a distinctive, deeply forked tail and blue back and wings.

Stan's Notes: A common and widespread swallow species in the state during summer and migration. It is common around bridges (especially bridges over water) and rural housing (especially in open country close to cliffs). Builds a gourd-shaped nest with a funnel-like entrance pointing down. Colony nester, with many nests lined up beneath eaves of buildings or under cliff overhangs. Will carry balls of mud up to a mile to construct its nest. Many of the colony return to the same nest sites each year. Not unusual for it to have two broods per season. If the number of nests under eaves becomes a problem, wait until after young have left nests to hose off mud.

BEWICK'S WREN
Thryomanes bewickii

Size: 5½" (14 cm)

Male: Brown cap, back, wings and tail. Gray chest and belly. White chin and eyebrows. Long tail with white spots on edges is cocked and flits sideways. Pointed down-curved bill.

Female: same as male

Juvenile: similar to adult

Nest: cavity; female and male build nest in woodpecker hole or nest box; 2-3 broods a year

Eggs: 4-8; white with brown markings

Incubation: 12-14 days; female incubates

Fledging: 10-14 days; female and male feed young

Migration: non-migrator to partial migrator; will move around to find food

Food: insects, seeds

Compare: House Wren (pg. 101) is slightly smaller and lacks the obvious white eyebrow marks and white spots on the tail.

Stan's Notes: A common wren of backyards and gardens. Insects make up 97 percent of its diet, with plant seeds composing the rest. Competes with House Wrens for nesting cavities. Male will choose nesting cavities and start to build nests using small uniform-sized sticks. Female will make the final selection of a nest site and finish building. Begins breeding in March and April. Has 2-3 broods per year. Male feeds female while she incubates. Average size territory per pair is 5 acres (2 ha), which they defend all year long.

male

female

YEAR-ROUND

HOUSE SPARROW
Passer domesticus

Size: 6" (15 cm)

Male: Medium sparrow-like bird with large black spot on throat extending down to the chest. Brown back and single white wing bars. A gray belly and crown.

Female: slightly smaller than the male, light brown, lacks the throat patch and single wing bars

Juvenile: similar to female

Nest: domed cup nest, within cavity; female and male build; 2-3 broods per year

Eggs: 4-6; white with brown markings

Incubation: 10-12 days; female incubates

Fledging: 14-17 days; female and male feed young

Migration: non-migrator; moves around to find food

Food: seeds, insects, fruit; comes to seed feeders

Compare: Lacks the rusty crown of Chipping Sparrow (pg. 107). Look for male House Sparrow's black bib. Female has a clear breast and no marking on head (cap).

Stan's Notes: One of the first bird songs heard in cities in spring. Familiar city bird, nearly always in small flocks. Introduced from Europe to Central Park, New York, in 1850. Now found throughout North America. These birds are not really sparrows, but members of the Weaver Finch family, characterized by their large, oversized domed nests. Constructs a nest containing scraps of plastic, paper and whatever else is available. An aggressive bird that will kill the young of other birds in order to take over a cavity.

winter pg. 267

breeding

LEAST SANDPIPER
Calidris minutilla

Size: 6" (15 cm)

Male: Breeding adult has golden brown head and back, and white eyebrows. White belly. Dull yellow legs. Short, down-curved black bill.

Female: same as male

Juvenile: similar to winter adult, but buff brown and lacking the breast band

Nest: ground; male and female construct; 1 brood per year

Eggs: 3-4; olive with dark markings

Incubation: 19-23 days; male and female incubate

Fledging: 25-28 days; male and female feed young

Migration: complete, to parts of California, Mexico and Central America

Food: aquatic and terrestrial insects, seeds

Compare: The smallest sandpiper species. Frequently confused with breeding Western Sandpiper (pg. 123). Least's yellow legs differentiate it from other tiny sandpipers. The short, thin, down-curved bill also helps to identify.

Stan's Notes: A winter resident in parts of California. The smallest of peeps (sandpipers) that nest on the tundra in northern regions of Canada and Alaska. Yellow legs can be hard to see in water, poor light or when covered with mud. Prefers grassy flats of saltwater and freshwater ponds. A tame sandpiper that can be approached without scaring.

winter pg. 269

breeding

WESTERN SANDPIPER
Calidris mauri

MIGRATION
WINTER

Size: 6½" (16 cm)

Male: Breeding has a bright rust brown crown, ear patch and back with white chin and chest. Black legs. Narrow bill that droops near tip.

Female: same as male

Juvenile: similar to breeding adult, bright buff brown on back only

Nest: ground; male and female construct; 1 brood per year

Eggs: 2-4; light brown with dark markings

Incubation: 20-22 days; male and female incubate

Fledging: 19-21 days; male and female feed young

Migration: complete, to coastal California, Mexico and Central America

Food: aquatic and terrestrial insects

Compare: Frequently is confused with breeding Least Sandpiper (pg. 121), but bright rust brown crown, ear patch and back help to identify. Look for black legs to differentiate from the Least Sandpiper. Western has a longer bill that droops slightly at tip.

Stan's Notes: A winter resident along coastal California and long-distance migrant. Nests on the ground in large "loose" colonies on the tundra of northern coastal Alaska. Adults leave their breeding grounds several weeks before young. Some obtain their breeding plumage before leaving California in spring. Feeds on insects at the water's edge, sometimes immersing its head. Young leave the nest (precocial) within a few hours after hatching. Female leaves and the male tends the hatchlings.

LARK SPARROW
Chondestes grammacus

YEAR-ROUND
MIGRATION
SUMMER
WINTER

Size: 6½" (16 cm)

Male: All-brown bird with unique rust red, white and black head pattern. White breast with a central black spot. Gray rump and white edges to gray tail, as seen in flight.

Female: same as male

Juvenile: similar to adult, no rust red on head

Nest: cup, on the ground; female builds; 1 brood per year

Eggs: 3-6; pale white with brown markings

Incubation: 10-12 days; male and female incubate

Fledging: 10-12 days; female and male feed young

Migration: non-migrator to complete in California

Food: seeds, insects

Compare: White-crowned Sparrow (pg. 127) lacks the Lark Sparrow's rust red pattern on the head and a central spot on a white breast. Larger than Chipping Sparrow (pg. 107), which has a similar rusty color on head, but lacks Lark's white breast and central spot.

Stan's Notes: One of the larger sparrow species and one of the best songsters, also well known for its courtship strutting, chasing and lark-like flight pattern (rapid wing beats with tail spread). A bird of open fields, pastures and prairies, found almost anywhere. Very common during migration, when large flocks congregate. Will use nest for several years if first brood is successful.

juvenile

WHITE-CROWNED SPARROW
Zonotrichia leucophrys

Size: 6½-7½" (16-19 cm)

Male: A brown sparrow with a gray breast and a black-and-white striped crown. Small, thin pink bill.

Female: same as male

Juvenile: similar to adult, with brown stripes on the head instead of white

Nest: cup; female builds; 2 broods per year

Eggs: 3-5; color varies from greenish to bluish to whitish with red brown markings

Incubation: 11-14 days; female incubates

Fledging: 8-12 days; male and female feed young

Migration: complete, to California and Mexico

Food: insects, seeds, berries; visits ground feeders

Compare: Black-throated Sparrow (pg. 263) is smaller and has a large black patch on throat. Lark Sparrow (pg. 125) has a rust red pattern on the head.

Stan's Notes: Winter visitor throughout California and year-round resident in parts of western California. Usually seen in groups of up to 20 during migration, when it feeds under seed feeders. A ground feeder, scratching backward with both feet at the same time. Males arrive before the females and establish territories by singing from perches. Nesting starts in April. Male takes the most responsibility for raising the young while the female starts a second brood. Only 9-12 days separate broods.

FOX SPARROW
Passerella iliaca

YEAR-ROUND
MIGRATION
SUMMER
WINTER

Size: 7" (18 cm)

Male: A plump brown sparrow with a gray head, back and rump. White chest and belly with rusty brown streaks. Rusty tail and wings.

Female: same as male

Juvenile: same as adult

Nest: cup; female builds; 2 broods per year

Eggs: 2-4; pale green with reddish markings

Incubation: 12-14 days; female incubates

Fledging: 10-11 days; female and male feed young

Migration: complete to non-migrator in California

Food: seeds, insects; comes to feeders

Compare: The Spotted Towhee (pg. 9) is found in a similar habitat, but the male Towhee has a black head.

Stan's Notes: One of the largest sparrows. Several color variations, depending upon the part of the country. Fox Sparrows in western states have gray heads and backs. Usually seen alone or in small groups, often beneath seed feeders looking for seeds and insects. Scratches like a chicken with both feet at the same time to find food. Constructs cup nest in brush on the ground and along forest edges. The common name "Sparrow" comes from the Anglo-Saxon word *spearwa*, meaning "flutterer," as applies to any small bird. "Fox" refers to the bird's rusty color.

male pg. 87

female

BLUE GROSBEAK
Passerina caerulea

MIGRATION
SUMMER

Size: 7" (18 cm)

Female: Overall brown with darker wings and tail. Two tan wing bars. Large gray-to-silver bill.

Male: blue bird with 2 chestnut wing bars, a large gray-to-silver bill, black around base of bill

Juvenile: similar to female

Nest: cup; female builds; 1-2 broods per year

Eggs: 3-6; pale blue without markings

Incubation: 11-12 days; female incubates

Fledging: 9-10 days; female and male feed young

Migration: complete, to Mexico and Central America

Food: insects, seeds; will come to seed feeders

Compare: Female Lazuli Bunting (pg. 113) is similar, but has 2 narrow white wing bars and is a lighter color overall.

Stan's Notes: This bird returns to California by early May. It has expanded northward with overall populations increasing over the past 30-40 years. A bird of semi-open habitats such as overgrown fields, riversides, woodland edges and fencerows. Frequently seen twitching and spreading its tail. First-year males show only some blue, obtaining the full complement of blue feathers in the second winter. Visits seed feeders.

HERMIT THRUSH
Catharus guttatus

YEAR-ROUND
MIGRATION
SUMMER
WINTER

Size: 7" (18 cm)

Male: Brown head, nape of neck and back with a heavily streaked or spotted white chest. Tail and edge of wings are rusty red. Thin white ring around each eye. Short thin bill. Often holds wings in a dropped position with tail cocked slightly upward.

Female: same as male

Juvenile: similar to adult

Nest: cup; female builds; 1-2 broods per year

Eggs: 3-6; greenish blue without markings

Incubation: 12-14 days; female incubates

Fledging: 12-14 days; female and male feed young

Migration: complete to non-migrator in California

Food: insects, fruit, spiders, earthworms

Compare: Smaller than California Thrasher (pg. 169), which has a long down-curved bill. Sage Thrasher (pg. 281) is lighter brown and lacks the rusty red tail and edge of wings.

Stan's Notes: A highly migratory thrush. Many live year-round in northwestern California. Northern birds join the resident birds in winter, increasing the population. Prefers mixed forest habitat and forest edges. Feeds mainly on the ground similar to the American Robin. Runs forward, stops and cocks its head, looking for movement. Frequently stands with its wings dropped down and rusty red tail cocked upward. Often raises and lowers tail, giving a soft clucking note after landing on a perch. Habitually flicks its wings when perched.

pale morph

HORNED LARK
Eremophila alpestris

YEAR-ROUND
MIGRATION

Size: 7-8" (18-20 cm)

Male: A sleek reddish tan bird with a yellow chin, black necklace and white lower breast and belly. Black bill. Two tiny "horns" on top of head can be difficult to see. A dark tail with white outer feathers, noticeable in flight.

Female: same as male, only duller, "horns" are even less noticeable

Juvenile: lacks reddish markings, black necklace and yellow chin, no "horns" until second year

Nest: ground; female builds; 2-3 broods per year

Eggs: 3-4; gray with brown markings

Incubation: 11-12 days; female incubates

Fledging: 9-12 days; female and male feed young

Migration: non-migrator in most of California

Food: seeds, insects

Compare: Smaller than Meadowlark (pg. 405), sharing the black necklace and yellow chin. Look for reddish marks and white lower chest.

Stan's Notes: Variable across the state from north to south. The only true lark native to North America. A bird of open ground. Common in rural areas. Often in large flocks. Moves about in winter to find food. Population increased in North America in the past century due to land clearing for farming. Starts to breed early in the year. Male performs a fluttering courtship flight high in the air while singing a high-pitched song. Female performs a fluttering distraction display if nest is disturbed. Can renest about seven days after brood fledges. "Lark" comes from the Middle English word *laverock*, or "a lark."

1 year old

Bohemian
Waxwing

CEDAR WAXWING
Bombycilla cedrorum

YEAR-ROUND
WINTER

Size: 7½" (19 cm)

Male: Very sleek-looking gray-to-brown bird with pointed crest, light yellow belly and bandit-like black mask. Tip of tail is bright yellow and the tips of wings look as if they have been dipped in red wax.

Female: same as male

Juvenile: grayish with a heavily streaked chest, lacks red wing tips, black mask and sleek look

Nest: cup; female and male build; 1 brood a year, occasionally 2

Eggs: 4-6; pale blue with brown markings

Incubation: 10-12 days; female incubates

Fledging: 14-18 days; female and male feed young

Migration: partial to non-migrator in California; moves around to find food

Food: cedar cones, fruit, insects

Compare: Similar to its larger, less common cousin, Bohemian Waxwing (see inset), which has white on wings and rust under tail.

Stan's Notes: The name is derived from its red wax-like wing tips and preference for eating small blueberry-like cones of the cedar. Mostly seen in flocks, moving from area to area, looking for berries. Wanders in winter to find available food supplies. During summer, before berries are abundant, it feeds on insects. Spends most of its time at the tops of tall trees. Listen for the very high-pitched "sreee" whistling sounds it constantly makes. Obtains mask after first year and red wing tips after second year. Usually a winter resident.

male pg. 5

female

BROWN-HEADED COWBIRD
Molothrus ater

YEAR-ROUND SUMMER

Size:	7½" (19 cm)
Female:	Dull brown bird with no obvious markings. Pointed, sharp gray bill.
Male:	glossy black bird, chocolate brown head
Juvenile:	similar to female, only dull gray color and a streaked chest
Nest:	no nest; lays eggs in nests of other birds
Eggs:	5-7; white with brown markings
Incubation:	10-13 days; host bird incubates eggs
Fledging:	10-11 days; host birds feed young
Migration:	non-migrator to partial in California
Food:	insects, seeds; will come to seed feeders
Compare:	Female Red-winged Blackbird (pg. 149) is slightly larger and has white eyebrows and a streaked chest. European Starling (pg. 3) has speckles and a shorter tail.

Stan's Notes: A member of the blackbird family. Of approximately 750 species of parasitic birds worldwide, this is the only parasitic bird in the state, laying eggs in host birds' nests, leaving others to raise its young. Cowbirds are known to have laid eggs in nests of over 200 species of birds. Some birds reject cowbird eggs, but most incubate them and raise the young, even to the exclusion of their own. Look for warblers and other birds feeding young birds twice their own size. At one time cowbirds followed bison to feed on insects attracted to the animals.

winter

breeding

SPOTTED SANDPIPER
Actitis macularius

YEAR-ROUND
MIGRATION
SUMMER
WINTER

Size: 8" (20 cm)

Male: Olive brown back. Long bill and long dull yellow legs. White line over eyes. Breeding plumage has black spots on a white chest and belly. Winter has a clear chest and belly.

Female: same as male

Juvenile: similar to winter adult, with a darker bill

Nest: ground; female and male build; 2 broods per year

Eggs: 3-4; brownish with brown markings

Incubation: 20-24 days; male incubates

Fledging: 17-21 days; male feeds young

Migration: complete, to southern California, Mexico, Central and South America

Food: aquatic insects

Compare: The Killdeer (pg. 165) has 2 black bands around neck. Look for Sandpiper to bob its tail up and down while standing. Look for breeding Spotted Sandpiper's black spots extending from chest to belly.

Stan's Notes: One of the few shorebirds that will dive underwater if pursued. Able to fly straight up out of the water. Flies with wings held in a cup-like arc, rarely lifting them above a horizontal plane. Constantly bobs its tail while standing and walks as if delicately balanced. Female mates with multiple males and lays eggs in up to five different nests. Male incubates and cares for young. Dramatic plumage change from breeding to winter. Lacks black spots on the chest and belly in winter.

winter pg. 275

breeding

SANDERLING
Calidris alba

WINTER

Size: 8" (20 cm)

Male: Breeding season (April to August) plumage has a rusty head, chest and back with white belly. Black legs and bill.

Female: same as male

Juvenile: spotty black on the head and back, a white belly, black legs and bill

Nest: ground; male builds; 1-2 broods per year

Eggs: 3-4; greenish olive with brown markings

Incubation: 24-30 days; male and female incubate

Fledging: 16-17 days; female and male feed young

Migration: complete, to coastal California, Mexico and Central and South America

Food: insects

Compare: Same size as the breeding plumage Spotted Sandpiper (pg. 141), but lacks chest spots.

Stan's Notes: One of the most common shorebirds in the state, but mostly seen in gray winter plumage from August to April. Can be seen in groups on sandy beaches, running out with each retreating wave to feed. Look for a flash of white on wings when it is in flight. Occasionally the female will mate with several males (polyandry), resulting in males and the female incubating separate nests. Both sexes will perform a distraction display if threatened. Nests on the Arctic tundra.

male pg. 351

female

BLACK-HEADED GROSBEAK
Pheucticus melanocephalus

MIGRATION
SUMMER

Size: 8" (20 cm)

Female: Appears like an overgrown sparrow. Overall brown with a lighter breast and belly. Large two-toned bill. Prominent white eyebrows. Yellow wing linings, as seen in flight.

Male: burnt orange chest, neck and rump, black head, tail and wings with irregular-shaped white wing patches, large bill with upper bill darker than lower

Juvenile: similar to adult of the same sex

Nest: cup; female builds; 1 brood per year

Eggs: 3-4; pale green or bluish, brown markings

Incubation: 11-13 days; female and male incubate

Fledging: 11-13 days; female and male feed young

Migration: complete, to Mexico, Central America and South America

Food: seeds, insects, fruit; comes to seed feeders

Compare: Female House Finch (pg. 105) is smaller, has more streaking on the chest and the bill isn't as large. Look for the female Grosbeak's unusual bicolored bill.

Stan's Notes: A cosmopolitan bird that nests in a wide variety of habitats. Both males and females sing and aggressively defend their nests against intruders. Song is very similar to the American Robin's and Western Tanager's, making it hard to tell them apart by song. Populations are increasing in California and across the U.S.

CACTUS WREN
Campylorhynchus brunneicapillus

YEAR-ROUND

Size: 8½" (22 cm)

Male: A large round-bodied wren with a long tail and a large, slightly downward curving bill. Bold white eyebrows and a chestnut brown crown. Many dark spots on upper breast to throat, often forming a central dark patch.

Female: same as male

Juvenile: similar to adult, shorter bill, lacks a spotty dark patch on breast

Nest: covered cup, domed or ball-shaped; female and male build; 2-3 broods per year

Eggs: 3-4; pale white to pink with brown marks

Incubation: 14-16 days; female incubates

Fledging: 19-23 days; female and male feed young

Migration: non-migrator

Food: insects, fruit, seeds; comes to seed feeders and water elements

Compare: Sage Thrasher (pg. 281) is gray and lacks a down-curving bill. Look for Cactus Wren's prominent white eyebrows to help identify.

Stan's Notes: Our largest wren. Backyard bird with a loud "krr-krr-krr-krr-krr" or "cha-cha-cha-cha." Male crouches, extends wings, fans tail and growls to female during courtship. Pairs stay together all year, defending territory. Builds a large nest usually in cholla or cactus, lining the chamber with grasses and feathers. Male builds another nest while female incubates first clutch of eggs. After the second brood fledges, roosts in nest during non-breeding season.

male pg. 11

female

RED-WINGED BLACKBIRD
Agelaius phoeniceus

YEAR-ROUND

Size: 8½" (22 cm)

Female: Heavily streaked brown bird with a pointed brown bill and white eyebrows.

Male: jet black bird with red and yellow patches on upper wings, pointed black bill

Juvenile: same as female

Nest: cup; female builds; 2-3 broods per year

Eggs: 3-4; bluish green with brown markings

Incubation: 10-12 days; female incubates

Fledging: 11-14 days; female and male feed young

Migration: non-migrator to partial migrator

Food: seeds, insects; will come to seed feeders

Compare: The female Tricolored Blackbird (pg. 151) is lighter brown and lacks the reddish tones. Female Yellow-headed Blackbird (pg. 161) and Brewer's Blackbird (pg. 153) are larger, Cowbird (pg. 139) is slightly smaller and all three lack the white eyebrows and heavily streaked chest of female Red-winged.

Stan's Notes: One of the most widespread and numerous birds in the state. It is a sure sign of spring when the Red-winged Blackbirds return to the marshes. Flocks of up to 100,000 birds have been reported. Males return before the females and defend territories by singing from tops of surrounding vegetation. Males repeat call from the tops of cattails while showing off their red and yellow wing bars (epaulets). Females choose mate and usually will nest over shallow water in thick stands of cattails. Red-wingeds feed mostly on seeds in fall and spring, switching to insects during summer.

male pg. 13

female

TRICOLORED BLACKBIRD
Agelaius tricolor

Size: 9" (22.5 cm)

Female: Overall dark brown with a gray chin and breast, a pointed dark bill and black legs. Dark reddish brown eyes.

Male: black with red and white shoulder patches (epaulets), pointed dark bill, dark reddish brown eyes

Juvenile: similar to female, but not as brown

Nest: cup; female builds; 2 broods per year

Eggs: 3-4; pale green with brown markings

Incubation: 11-13 days; female incubates

Fledging: 11-14 days; female and male feed young

Migration: non-migrator to partial migrator; will move around to find food

Food: insects, seeds, grain; visits ground feeders

Compare: The female Red-winged Blackbird (pg. 149) is darker brown with reddish tones.

Stan's Notes: Blackbird species found mainly in California. Very closely related to Red-winged Blackbirds. Tricolored usually has a smaller bill than Red-winged. Flocks with Red-wingeds and other blackbirds during winter, moving around to find food and nesting colonies. Sometimes moves from one area to another for unknown reasons. Tricoloreds and Red-wingeds have some of the highest nesting densities of any bird species, with some colonies in the tens of thousands. Like the Red-winged, it nests in shallow freshwater marshes. Builds nest from woven sedges, grasses and other green plants. Attaches nest to upright cattail stems and lines it with finer plant fibers. Young are fed mainly insects.

male pg. 15

female

BREWER'S BLACKBIRD
Euphagus cyanocephalus

YEAR-ROUND
SUMMER
WINTER

Size: 9" (22.5 cm)

Female: An overall grayish brown bird. Legs and bill nearly black. While most have dark eyes, some have bright white or pale yellow eyes.

Male: glossy black, shining green in direct light, head purplish, white or pale yellow eyes

Juvenile: similar to female

Nest: cup; female builds; 1-2 broods per year

Eggs: 4-6; gray with brown markings

Incubation: 12-14 days; female incubates

Fledging: 13-14 days; female and male feed young

Migration: non-migrator to partial in California; moves around to find food

Food: insects, seeds, fruit

Compare: Larger in size and darker in color than the female Brown-headed Cowbird (pg. 139). Female Red-winged Blackbird (pg. 149) is similar in size, but has a heavily streaked chest and prominent white eyebrows.

Stan's Notes: Common blackbird often found in association with agricultural lands and seen in open areas such as wet pastures and mountain meadows up to 10,000 feet (3,050 m). Male and some females are easily identified by their bright, nearly white eyes. It is a common cowbird host, usually nesting in a shrub, small tree or directly on the ground. Prefers to nest in small colonies of up to 20 pairs. Gathers in large flocks with cowbirds, Red-wingeds and other blackbirds to migrate. It is expanding its range in North America.

CALIFORNIA TOWHEE
Pipilo crissalis

Size: 9" (22.5 cm)

Male: Overall light brown to gray with faint dark streaks. Lighter brown throat. Rusty brown just under base of tail. Long tail. Short bill.

Female: same as male

Juvenile: similar to adult

Nest: cup; female builds; 1-2 broods per year

Eggs: 2-6; pale blue with dark markings

Incubation: 11-14 days; female incubates

Fledging: 12-14 days; female and male feed young

Migration: non-migrator

Food: seeds, insects, fruit; visits ground feeders

Compare: Larger than Green-tailed Towhee (pg. 329), which has a rusty red cap and bright white chin and throat. The female Spotted Towhee (pg. 9) is smaller with rusty red sides and a white chest and belly.

Stan's Notes: A stocky bird that tends to remain in or near heavy brush or shrubs, but is common in suburban areas. Comes out in the open to feed. Dashes back at any disturbance. Usually seen on the ground foraging for seeds and insects. Comes to seeds on the ground scattered under a backyard feeder. Often seen in pairs and can be very tame in some places. Until recently, California Towhee and Canyon Towhee (not shown) were one species, called Brown Towhee. California Towhee is found only in California and in Baja California, Mexico. The Canyon Towhee is found in Arizona, New Mexico and Texas. Their ranges rarely overlap.

female

male

COMMON NIGHTHAWK
Chordeiles minor

Size: 9" (22.5 cm)

Male: A camouflaged brown and white bird with white chin. A distinctive white band across wings and the tail, seen only in flight.

Female: similar to male, but with tan chin, lacks the white tail band

Juvenile: similar to female

Nest: no nest; lays eggs on the ground, usually on rocks, or on rooftop; 1 brood per year

Eggs: 2; cream with lavender markings

Incubation: 19-20 days; female and male incubate

Fledging: 20-21 days; female and male feed young

Migration: complete, to South America

Food: insects caught in air

Compare: Look for the obvious white wing band of the Nighthawk in flight and characteristic flap-flap-flap-glide flight pattern.

Stan's Notes: Usually only seen flying at dusk or after sunset, but not uncommon for it to be sitting on a fence post, sleeping during the day. A very noisy bird, repeating a "peenting" call during flight. Alternates slow wing beats with bursts of quick wing beats. Prolific insect eater. Prefers gravel rooftops for nesting in cities and nests on the ground in country. Male's distinctive springtime mating ritual is a steep diving flight terminated with a loud popping noise. One of the first birds to migrate each fall, starting in August. A summer resident in parts of northern California. Usually seen only during migration in the rest of the state.

BURROWING OWL
Athene cunicularia

Size: 9½" (24 cm); up to 21-inch wingspan

Male: A brown owl with bold white spots, white belly and very long legs. Yellow eyes.

Female: same as male

Juvenile: same as adult, but belly is brown

Nest: cavity, former underground mammal den; female and male line den; 1 brood per year

Eggs: 6-11; white without markings

Incubation: 21-28 days; female incubates

Fledging: 25-28 days; female and male feed young

Migration: non-migrator to partial in California

Food: insects, mammals, lizards, birds

Compare: Western Screech-Owl (pg. 283) is slightly smaller and has ear tufts. Burrowing Owl is less than half the size of Great Horned Owl (pg. 231), which has feather tuft "horns." Burrowing spends most of its time on the ground unlike tree-loving Great Horned.

Stan's Notes: An owl of fields, open backyards, golf courses and airports. Nests in small family units or in small colonies. Takes over the underground dens of mammals, occasionally widening its den by kicking dirt backward. Lines den with cow pies, horse dung, grass and feathers. Some people have had success attracting these owls to their backyards by creating artificial dens. Often seen in the day, standing or sleeping around den entrance. Male brings food to incubating female, often moving family to a new den when young are just a few weeks old. Will bob head up and down while doing deep knee bends when agitated or threatened.

male pg. 17

female

YELLOW-HEADED BLACKBIRD
Xanthocephalus xanthocephalus

YEAR-ROUND
MIGRATION
SUMMER
WINTER

Size: 9-11" (22.5-28 cm)

Female: A large brown bird with a dull yellow head and chest. Slightly smaller than male.

Male: black bird with a lemon yellow head, chest and nape of neck, black mask and gray bill, white wing patches

Juvenile: similar to female

Nest: cup; female builds; 2 broods per year

Eggs: 3-5; greenish white with brown markings

Incubation: 11-13 days; female incubates

Fledging: 9-12 days; female feeds young

Migration: complete, to parts of California, Mexico

Food: insects, seeds; will come to ground feeders

Compare: Larger than female Red-winged Blackbird (pg. 149), which has white eyebrows and a streaked chest.

Stan's Notes: Usually heard before seen, Yellow-headed Blackbird has a low, hoarse, raspy or metallic call. Nests in deep water marshes unlike its cousin, the Red-winged Blackbird, which prefers shallow water. The male gives an impressive mating display, flying with head drooped and feet and tail pointing down while steadily beating its wings. The female incubates alone and feeds 3-5 young. Young keep low and out of sight for as many as three weeks before starting to fly. Migrates in flocks of up to 200 with other blackbirds. Flocks made up mainly of males return first in early April; females return later. Most colonies consist of 20-100 nests.

male

female

AMERICAN KESTREL
Falco sparverius

Size: 10-12" (25-30 cm); up to 2-foot wingspan

Male: Rusty brown back and tail. A white breast with dark spots. Double black vertical lines on white face. Blue gray wings. Distinctive wide black band with a white edge on tip of rusty tail.

Female: similar to male, but slightly larger, has rusty brown wings and dark bands on tail

Juvenile: same as adult of the same sex

Nest: cavity; doesn't build a nest within; 1 brood per year

Eggs: 4-5; white with brown markings

Incubation: 29-31 days; male and female incubate

Fledging: 30-31 days; female and male feed young

Migration: non-migrator in California

Food: insects, small mammals and birds, reptiles

Compare: Similar to other falcons. Look for 2 vertical black stripes on the Kestrel's face. No other small bird of prey has a rusty back and tail.

Stan's Notes: A falcon that was once called Sparrow Hawk due to its small size. Could be called Grasshopper Hawk because it eats many grasshoppers. Hovers close to roads before diving for prey. Adapts quickly to a wooden nesting box. Has pointed swept-back wings, seen in flight. Perches nearly upright. Unusual raptor in that males and females have quite different markings. Watch for them to pump their tails up and down after landing on perches.

KILLDEER
Charadrius vociferus

**YEAR-ROUND
SUMMER**

Size: 11" (28 cm)

Male: An upland shorebird that has 2 black bands around the neck like a necklace. A brown back and white belly. Bright reddish orange rump, visible in flight.

Female: same as male

Juvenile: similar to adult, with 1 neck band

Nest: ground; male builds; 2 broods per year

Eggs: 3-5; tan with brown markings

Incubation: 24-28 days; male and female incubate

Fledging: 25 days; male and female lead their young to food

Migration: non-migrator in California

Food: insects

Compare: The Spotted Sandpiper (pg. 141) is found around water and lacks the 2 neck bands of the Killdeer.

Stan's Notes: The only shorebird with two black neck bands. It is known for its broken wing impression, which draws intruders away from nest. Once clear of the nest, the Killdeer takes flight. Nests are only a slight depression in a gravel area, often very difficult to see. Young look like yellow cotton balls on stilts when first hatched, but quickly molt to appear similar to parents. Able to follow parents and peck for insects soon after birth. Is technically classified as a shorebird, but doesn't live at the shore. Often found in vacant fields or along railroads. Has a very distinctive "kill-deer" call.

red-shafted male

red-shafted female

NORTHERN FLICKER
Colaptes auratus

Size: 12" (30 cm)

Male: Brown and black woodpecker with a large white rump patch visible only when flying. Black necklace above a speckled chest. Gray head with a brown cap. Red mustache.

Female: same as male, but lacks the red mustache

Juvenile: same as adult of the same sex

Nest: cavity; female and male excavate; 1 brood per year

Eggs: 5-8; white without markings

Incubation: 11-14 days; female and male incubate

Fledging: 25-28 days; female and male feed young

Migration: non-migrator to partial in California

Food: insects, especially ants and beetles

Compare: Female Williamson's Sapsucker (pg. 47) has a finely barred back with a yellow belly and lacks Flicker's black spots on chest and belly. Look for Flicker's speckled breast and gray head to help identify.

Stan's Notes: The flicker is the only woodpecker to regularly feed on the ground, preferring ants and beetles. Produces antacid saliva to neutralize the acidic defense of ants. Male usually selects a nest site, taking up to 12 days to excavate. Some have been successful attracting flickers to nest boxes stuffed with sawdust. During flight, flashes reddish orange under the wings and tail. Undulates deeply and gives a loud "wacka-wacka" call when in flight.

CALIFORNIA THRASHER
Toxostoma redivivum

YEAR-ROUND

Size: 12" (30 cm)

Male: Overall light brown. A rusty wash to lower chest, belly and rump. Long, down-curved dark bill with a white chin and several dark lines that run just below the eyes and across the face. Dark eyes. Long tail.

Female: same as male

Juvenile: similar to adult

Nest: cup; male and female construct; 1-2 broods per year

Eggs: 2-4; pale blue with brown markings

Incubation: 12-14 days; female and male incubate

Fledging: 12-14 days; female and male feed young

Migration: non-migrator

Food: insects, fruit, nuts, small lizards; will come to feeders and birdbaths

Compare: Much larger than Sage Thrasher (pg. 281), which has a streaked breast and belly and lacks the long down-curved bill.

Stan's Notes: Unique to California (endemic). Likes dense brush. Forages on the ground for food, sweeping bill back and forth like a rake to uncover it. Eats seeds under feeders in suburban areas. Often runs with tail cocked up. Often heard before seen. Male sings from perches while female remains hidden. Mimics other birds, repeating phrases and interspersing with low, harsh notes. Female flutters her wings and begs for food in response. Male cares for fledglings while female lays eggs for a second brood. Unable to fly for several days, fledglings follow male around on the ground, learning what to eat.

YEAR-ROUND

MOURNING DOVE
Zenaida macroura

Size: 12" (30 cm)

Male: Smooth fawn-colored dove with gray patch on the head. Iridescent pink, green around neck. A single black spot behind and below eyes. Black spots on wings and tail. Pointed wedge-shaped tail with white edges.

Female: similar to male, lacking iridescent pink and green neck feathers

Juvenile: spotted and streaked

Nest: platform; female and male build; 2 broods per year

Eggs: 2; white without markings

Incubation: 13-14 days; male and female incubate, the male during day, female at night

Fledging: 12-14 days; female and male feed young

Migration: non-migrator to partial migrator; will move around to find food

Food: seeds; will visit seed and ground feeders

Compare: Spotted Dove (pg. 173) is not as common and widespread. Rock Pigeon (pg. 301) has a wide range of color combinations.

Stan's Notes: Name comes from its mournful cooing. A ground feeder, bobbing its head as it walks. One of the few birds to drink without lifting its head, same as Rock Pigeon. Parents feed young (squab) a regurgitated liquid called crop-milk the first few days of life. Flimsy platform nest of twigs often falls apart during a storm. Wind rushing through wing feathers during flight creates a characteristic whistling sound.

SPOTTED DOVE
Streptopelia chinensis

YEAR-ROUND

Size: 12" (30 cm)

Male: Dark reddish brown with a gray head and lower belly. Distinct black and white spots on nape, like tiny scales. Some have a large scalloped pattern on back and wings. Large rounded tail with a white tip.

Female: same as male

Juvenile: similar to adult, lacks black and white spots on nape of neck

Nest: platform; female and male build; 1 brood per year

Eggs: 2-4; pale green to white without markings

Incubation: 12-14 days; female incubates

Fledging: 12-14 days; female and male feed young

Migration: non-migrator; moves around to find food

Food: seeds, fruit, insects; visits ground feeders

Compare: Mourning Dove (pg. 171) is much more common and widespread. Mourning Dove and juvenile Spotted Dove both lack spots on nape and are easy to confuse.

Stan's Notes: A non-native, usually in suburban yards in southern California. Often associated with eucalyptus trees. Frequently seen feeding on spilled seeds beneath feeders. Apparently intentionally released in the past, it has joined escaped birds from the pet trade. Now well established in several areas. Juveniles lack spots on nape, making it easy to confuse with Mourning Doves. To distinguish the two, look at the tail. Spotted Dove has a larger, rounded tail with a white tip. Mourning Dove's tail is pointed with white edges.

PIED-BILLED GREBE
Podilymbus podiceps

YEAR-ROUND

Size: 13" (33 cm)

Male: Small brown water bird with a black chin and black ring around a thick, chicken-like ivory bill. Puffy white patch under the tail. Has an unmarked brown bill during winter (September to February).

Female: same as male

Juvenile: paler than adult, with white spots and gray chest, belly and bill

Nest: floating platform; female and male build; 1 brood per year

Eggs: 5-7; bluish white without markings

Incubation: 22-24 days; female and male incubate

Fledging: 22-24 days; female and male feed young

Migration: non-migrator in California

Food: crayfish, aquatic insects, fish

Compare: The smallest brown water bird that dives underwater for long periods of time.

Stan's Notes: Common resident grebe, often seen diving for food. Slowly sinks like a submarine if disturbed. Sinks without diving by quickly compressing feathers to force air out. Was called Hell-diver because of the length of time it can stay submerged. Can surface far from where it went under. Very sensitive to pollution. Adapted well to life on water, with short wings, lobed toes, and legs set close to rear of body. While swimming is easy, it is very awkward on land. Builds nest on a floating mat in water. "Grebe" probably came from the Old English *krib*, meaning "crest," a reference to the crested head plumes of many grebes, especially during breeding season.

male pg. 53

female

BUFFLEHEAD
Bucephala albeola

Size: 13-15" (33-38 cm)

Female: Brownish gray duck with dark brown head. White patch on cheek, just behind eyes.

Male: striking black and white duck with a head that shines green purple in sunlight, large white bonnet-like patch on back of head

Juvenile: similar to female

Nest: cavity; female lines old woodpecker cavity; 1 brood per year

Eggs: 8-10; ivory to olive without markings

Incubation: 29-31 days; female incubates

Fledging: 50-55 days; female leads young to food

Migration: complete, to California, Mexico and Central America

Food: aquatic insects

Compare: Commonly confused with female Common Goldeneye (pg. 209), which lacks the white cheek patch. Slightly smaller than female Lesser Scaup (pg. 193), which has a white patch at base of bill.

Stan's Notes: Common diving duck that travels with other ducks. Seen during migration and throughout winter, arriving in the state late in August. Found on rivers and lakes. Nests in old woodpecker cavities. Unlike other ducks, young stay in nests for up to two days before venturing out with their mothers. Female is very territorial and remains with the same mate for many years.

GREATER YELLOWLEGS
Tringa melanoleuca

Size: 14" (36 cm)

Male: Tall bird with a bulbous head and long thin bill, slightly turned up. Gray streaking on chest. White belly. Long yellow legs.

Female: same as male

Juvenile: same as adult

Nest: ground; female builds; 1 brood per year

Eggs: 3-4; off-white with brown markings

Incubation: 22-23 days; female and male incubate

Fledging: 18-20 days; male and female feed young

Migration: complete, to California, Mexico and Central and South America

Food: small fish, aquatic insects

Compare: Similar in size to breeding Willet (pg. 183), with a longer neck, smaller head and bright yellow legs. Greater Yellowlegs is an overall more brown bird than breeding Willet.

Stan's Notes: A common winter shorebird that can be identified by the slightly upturned bill and long yellow legs. Frequently seen resting on one leg. Its long legs carry it through deep water. Feeds by rushing forward through the water, plowing its bill or swinging it from side to side, catching small fish and insects. A skittish bird quick to give an alarm call, causing flocks to take flight. Quite often moves into the water prior to taking flight. Has a variety of "flight" notes that it gives when taking off. Nests on the ground near water on the northern tundra of Labrador and Newfoundland.

male pg. 25

female

YEAR-ROUND

GREAT-TAILED GRACKLE
Quiscalus mexicanus

Size: 15" (38 cm), female
18" (45 cm), male

Female: An overall brown bird with gray-to-brown belly. Light brown-to-white eyes, eyebrows, throat and upper portion of chest.

Male: all-black bird with iridescent purple sheen on head and back, exceptionally long tail, bright yellow eyes

Juvenile: similar to female

Nest: cup; female builds; 1-2 broods per year

Eggs: 3-5; greenish blue with brown markings

Incubation: 12-14 days; female incubates

Fledging: 21-23 days; female feeds young

Migration: non-migrator to partial in California; moves around to find food

Food: insects, fruit, seeds; comes to seed feeders

Compare: Larger than the female Brewer's Blackbird (pg. 153), with a much lighter brown chest and distinct light brown eyebrows.

Stan's Notes: This is our largest grackle. It was once considered a subspecies of the Boat-tailed Grackle, which occurs along the East coast and Florida. A bird that prefers to nest near water in an open habitat. A colony nester, males do not participate in nest building, incubation or raising of young. Males rarely fight, but females will squabble over nest sites and materials. Several females mate with one male. They are expanding northward, moving into northern states. Western populations tend to be larger than the eastern. Song varies from population to population.

breeding

winter pg. 305

displaying

WILLET
Catoptrophorus semipalmatus

SUMMER
WINTER

Size: 15" (38 cm)

Male: Brown breeding plumage with a brown bill and legs. White belly. Distinctive black and white wing lining pattern, seen in flight or during display.

Female: same as male

Juvenile: similar to breeding adult, more tan in color

Nest: ground; female builds; 1 brood per year

Eggs: 3-5; olive green with dark markings

Incubation: 24-28 days; male and female incubate

Fledging: unknown days; female and male feed young

Migration: complete, to parts of California, the coast of Mexico, Central and South America

Food: aquatic insects

Compare: Slightly larger than the Greater Yellowlegs (pg. 179), which has yellow legs. Marbled Godwit (pg. 203) is larger and has a two-toned, upturned bill.

Stan's Notes: A common winter resident in California. Northern birds pass through coastal California to destinations farther south. Appearing a rich, warm brown during breeding season and rather plain gray in winter, it always has a striking black and white wing pattern when seen in flight. Uses its black and white wing patches to display to its mate. Named after the "pill-will-willet" call it gives during the breeding season. Gives a "kip-kip-kip" alarm call when it takes flight. It nests in far northeastern California, other western states, along the East coast and in Canada.

winter male

male

female

RUDDY DUCK
Oxyura jamaicensis

YEAR-ROUND

Size: 15" (38 cm)

Male: Compact reddish brown body with a black crown and nape. Large bright white cheek patch. Distinctive light blue bill. Long tail, often raised above water. Winter has a dull brown-to-gray body and dark bill.

Female: similar to winter male, lacks the large white cheek patch and blue bill

Juvenile: similar to female

Nest: ground; female builds; 1 brood per year

Eggs: 6-8; pale white without markings

Incubation: 23-26 days; female incubates

Fledging: 42-48 days; female and male feed young

Migration: partial to non-migrator; moves to find food

Food: aquatic insects and plants

Compare: Male Goldeneye (pg. 67) has mostly white sides and a green head. Female Goldeneye (pg. 209) has bright yellow eyes and a light gray body. Male Ring-necked Duck (pg. 61) has gray sides and a white outline on bill.

Stan's Notes: A diving duck with a unique appearance. Awkward on land. Often secretive, found on ponds and bays. Flushes quickly and stays away for a long time. Breeding male displays like a windup toy, ratcheting his head up and down, making muffled sounds and a staccato "pop." Male breeds with more than one female. Female lays some eggs in other duck nests. Male often seen with female and ducklings, but is not the father. Babies can dive soon after hatching. Has a blue bill, but is not the species that duck hunters call Blue Bill.

male

female

GREEN-WINGED TEAL
Anas crecca

WINTER

Size: 15" (38 cm)

Male: A chestnut head with a dark green patch in back of eyes extending down to the nape of neck and outlined in white. Gray body with a butter yellow tail. Green speculum.

Female: light brown in color with black spots, green speculum, small black bill

Juvenile: same as female

Nest: ground; female builds; 1 brood per year

Eggs: 8-10; creamy white without markings

Incubation: 21-23 days; female incubates

Fledging: 32-34 days; female teaches young to feed

Migration: complete, to California

Food: aquatic plants and insects

Compare: Male Green-winged is not as colorful as the male Wood Duck (pg. 333). Female Green-winged is very similar to the larger female Cinnamon Teal (pg. 191), which lacks the dark line through eyes and has a larger bill. The female Blue-winged Teal (pg. 189) is similar in size and has a slight white mark at base of bill.

Stan's Notes: One of the smallest dabbling ducks, it tips forward in the water to feed off the bottom of shallow ponds. This behavior makes it vulnerable to ingesting spent lead shot, which can cause death. It walks well on land and also feeds in fields and woodlands. Known for its fast and agile flight, groups spin and wheel through the air in tight formation. Green speculum most obvious in flight.

male

female

BLUE-WINGED TEAL
Anas discors

MIGRATION
SUMMER
WINTER

Size: 15-16" (38-40 cm)

Male: Small, plain-looking brown duck speckled with black. A gray head with a large white crescent-shaped mark at base of bill. Black tail with small white patch. Blue wing patch (speculum) usually seen only in flight.

Female: duller version of male, lacks facial crescent mark and white patch on tail, showing only slight white at base of bill

Juvenile: same as female

Nest: ground; female builds; 1 brood per year

Eggs: 8-11; creamy white

Incubation: 23-27 days; female incubates

Fledging: 35-44 days; female feeds young

Migration: complete, to California, Mexico and Central America

Food: aquatic plants, seeds, aquatic insects

Compare: Male Blue-winged has a distinct white face marking. The female Blue-winged is smaller than the female Mallard (pg. 211). Female Green-winged Teal (pg. 187) has a similar size, but lacks white at base of bill.

Stan's Notes: One of the smallest ducks in North America. Nests some distance from water. Female performs a distraction display to protect nest and young. Male leaves female near end of incubation. Planting crops and cultivating to pond edges have caused a decline in population. Widespread nesting, breeding as far north as Alaska. One of the longest distance migrating ducks.

male

female

CINNAMON TEAL
Anas cyanoptera

Size: 16" (40 cm)

Male: Deep cinnamon head, neck and belly. Light brown back. Dark gray bill. Deep red eyes. Non-breeding (July to September) male is overall brown with a red tinge.

Female: overall brown with a pale brown head, long shovel-like bill, green patch on wings

Juvenile: similar to female

Nest: ground; female builds; 1 brood per year

Eggs: 7-12; pinkish white without markings

Incubation: 21-25 days; female incubates

Fledging: 40-50 days; female teaches young to feed

Migration: non-migrator to partial in California

Food: aquatic plants and insects, seeds

Compare: Male Teal shares the cinnamon sides of the larger male Northern Shoveler (pg. 339), but lacks Shoveler's green head and very large spoon-shaped bill. Female Cinnamon Teal looks very similar to the smaller female Green-winged Teal (pg. 187), which has a dark line through the eyes.

Stan's Notes: The male teal is one of the most stunningly beautiful ducks. When threatened, the female feigns a wing injury to lure predators away from young. Prefers to nest along alkaline marshes and shallow lakes, within 75 yards (68 m) of water. Mallards and other ducks often lay eggs in teal nests, resulting in many nests totaling over 15 eggs.

male pg. 59

female

LESSER SCAUP
Aythya affinis

YEAR-ROUND
MIGRATION
WINTER

Size: 16-17" (40-43 cm)

Female: Overall brown duck with dull white patch at base of light gray bill. Yellow eyes.

Male: white and gray, the chest and head appear nearly black but head appears purple with green highlights in direct sun, yellow eyes

Juvenile: same as female

Nest: ground; female builds; 1 brood per year

Eggs: 8-14; olive buff without markings

Incubation: 22-28 days; female incubates

Fledging: 45-50 days; female teaches young to feed

Migration: complete, to California, Mexico, Central America and northern South America

Food: aquatic plants and insects

Compare: Similar size as the female Ring-necked Duck (pg. 197), but lacking the white ring around the bill. Male Blue-winged Teal (pg. 189) is slightly smaller and has a crescent-shaped white mark at the base of bill. The female Wood Duck (pg. 205) is larger with white around the eyes.

Stan's Notes: A common diving duck. Often seen in large flocks on lakes, ponds and sewage lagoons. Completely submerges itself to feed on the bottom of lakes (unlike dabbling ducks, which only tip forward to reach the bottom). Note the bold white stripe under the wings when in flight. Has an interesting baby-sitting arrangement in which groups of young are tended by 1-3 adult females. A winter resident. Doesn't breed in most of California.

soaring

RED-SHOULDERED HAWK
Buteo lineatus

**YEAR-ROUND
WINTER**

Size: 15-19" (38-48 cm); up to 3½-foot wingspan

Male: Orange-to-red (cinnamon) head, shoulders, chest and belly. Wings and back are nearly black with white spots. Thin white bands and wide black bands on tail. Obvious red wing linings, seen in flight.

Female: same as male

Juvenile: similar to adult, with a brownish red head, chest and wing linings

Nest: platform; female and male build; 1 brood per year

Eggs: 2-4; white with dark markings

Incubation: 27-29 days; female and male incubate

Fledging: 39-45 days; female and male feed young

Migration: non-migrator to partial migrator

Food: reptiles, amphibians, large insects, birds

Compare: The Red-tailed (pg. 221) has a white chest. Cooper's (pg. 307) has a slimmer body and longer tail. Sharp-shinned Hawk (pg. 299) lacks a reddish head and belly. Look for the cinnamon head, shoulders, chest and belly.

Stan's Notes: Common in woodlands and backyards in the state. Prefers to hunt along forest edges, spotting snakes, frogs, insects, an occasional small bird and other prey while perching. Often seen flapping with an alternating gliding pattern. Very vocal. A distinct scream. Mates when 2-3 years old. Stays in same territory for many years. Starts building nest in February. Young leave nest by June.

male pg. 61

female

RING-NECKED DUCK
Aythya collaris

Size: 17" (43 cm)

Female: Mainly brown back with light brown sides, a gray face and dark brown crown. White eye-ring extends into a line behind eyes. A white ring around a light blue bill. Top of head is peaked.

Male: black head, breast and back, sides are gray to nearly white, a bold white ring around a light blue bill and second ring at the base of bill, top of head is peaked

Juvenile: similar to female

Nest: ground; female builds; 1 brood per year

Eggs: 8-10; olive gray to brown without markings

Incubation: 26-27 days; female incubates

Fledging: 49-56 days; female teaches young to feed

Migration: complete, to California, Mexico and Central America

Food: aquatic plants and insects

Compare: Female Lesser Scaup (pg. 193) is similar in size. Look for female Ring-necked's white ring around the bill.

Stan's Notes: Common winter duck throughout the state. A diving duck, watch for it to dive underwater to forage for food. Takes to flight by springing up off water. Was named "Ring-necked" because of the cinnamon collar (nearly impossible to see in the field). Also called Ring-billed Duck due to the white ring on its bill.

male pg. 63

female

HOODED MERGANSER
Lophodytes cucullatus

WINTER

Size: 16-19" (40-48 cm)

Female: Sleek brown and rust bird with a red head. Ragged "hair" on back of head. Long, thin brown bill.

Male: same size and shape as female, but a black back and rust sides, crest "hood" raises to reveal large white patch, long black bill

Juvenile: similar to female

Nest: cavity; female lines old woodpecker hole; 1 brood per year

Eggs: 10-12; white without markings

Incubation: 32-33 days; female incubates

Fledging: 71 days; female feeds young

Migration: complete, to northwestern California

Food: small fish, aquatic insects

Compare: Very similar to, but smaller than, the female Red-breasted Merganser (pg. 229), which has a larger, lighter-colored bill. Larger than female Lesser Scaup (pg. 193), which has a dull white patch at base of bill.

Stan's Notes: A small diving bird of shallow-water ponds, sloughs, lakes and rivers. Rarely found away from wooded areas, where it nests in natural cavities or nest boxes. The female will "dump" eggs into other female Hooded Merganser nests, resulting in 20-25 eggs in some nests. Known to share a nesting cavity with a Wood Duck, sitting side by side. Male Hooded Merganser can voluntarily raise and lower its crest to show off the white head patch.

WHIMBREL
Numenius phaeopus

MIGRATION
WINTER

Size: 18" (45 cm)

Male: Heavily streaked bird, light brown to gray. A long down-curved bill and multiple dark brown stripes on crown. Dark line through eyes. Legs are light gray to blue.

Female: same as male

Juvenile: similar to adult

Nest: ground; female and male construct; 1 brood per year

Eggs: 3-4; olive green with dark markings

Incubation: 27-28 days; male and female incubate

Fledging: 35-42 days; female and male feed young

Migration: complete, to coastal California, Mexico and Central and South America

Food: insects, snails, worms, leeches, berries

Compare: Larger than the breeding Willet (pg. 183). Same size as the Marbled Godwit (pg. 203), which has an upturned bill compared with Whimbrel's down-curved bill.

Stan's Notes: Mostly a winter resident, easily identified by its very long down-curved bill and brown stripes on head. Uses its bill to probe deep into sand and mud for insects. Unlike other shorebirds, berries become an important food source in summer. Is very vocal, giving single note whistles. Returns to tundra of northern Alaska to nest. Doesn't breed until age 3. Has a long-term pair bond. Adults leave breeding grounds up to two weeks before the young leave.

MARBLED GODWIT
Limosa fedoa

WINTER

Size: 18" (45 cm)

Male: A tawny brown overall with a darker back. Long, two-toned and slightly upturned bill with black tip and pinkish base. Long gray legs. Cinnamon under wings, seen in flight.

Female: same as male

Juvenile: similar to adult

Nest: ground; female and male construct; 1 brood per year

Eggs: 3-5; olive green with dark markings

Incubation: 21-23 days; male and female incubate

Fledging: 20-21 days; female and male feed young

Migration: complete, to coastal California, Mexico and Central America

Food: aquatic insects, snails, worms, leeches

Compare: Larger than the breeding Willet (pg. 183). Same size as the Whimbrel (pg. 201), which has a down-curved bill compared with the slightly upturned bill of the Godwit.

Stan's Notes: A winter resident that is easily identified by its very long, two-toned, slightly upturned bill. Uses its bill to probe deep into sand and mud for insects. Usually feeds in mid-thigh water. In the winter, prefers saltwater beaches and mud flats up and down the West coast. Returns to Prairie Pothole regions of North Dakota and Canada for nesting. Nests in short grass prairie near wetlands. Overall population is declining. Name comes from its "godWHIT-godWHIT" call.

male pg. 333

female

WOOD DUCK
Aix sponsa

YEAR-ROUND
SUMMER
WINTER

Size: 17-20" (43-50 cm)

Female: A small brown dabbling duck. Bright white eye-ring and a not-so-obvious crest. A blue patch on wing is often hidden.

Male: highly ornamented with a green head and crest patterned with white and black, rusty chest, white belly and red eyes

Juvenile: same as female

Nest: cavity; female lines old woodpecker cavity; 1 brood per year

Eggs: 10-15; creamy white without markings

Incubation: 28-36 days; female incubates

Fledging: 56-68 days; female teaches young to feed

Migration: non-migrator to partial in California

Food: aquatic insects, plants, seeds

Compare: Female Mallard (pg. 211) and female Blue-winged Teal (pg. 189) lack the bright white eye-ring and crest. The female Northern Shoveler (pg. 217) is larger and has a large spoon-shaped bill.

Stan's Notes: A common duck of quiet, shallow backwater ponds. Nests in old woodpecker holes or in nest boxes. Often seen flying deep in forests or perched high on tree branches. Female takes to flight with a loud squealing call, entering nest cavity from full flight. Will lay eggs in a neighboring female nest (egg dumping), resulting in some clutches in excess of 20 eggs. Young stay in nest cavity only 24 hours after hatching, then jump from up to 30 feet (9 m) to the ground or water to follow their mother, never returning to the nest.

male pg. 359

female

REDHEAD
Aythya americana

YEAR-ROUND
WINTER

Size: 19" (48 cm)

Female: Plain, soft brown duck with gray-to-white wing linings. Top of head is rounded. Two-toned bill, gray with a black tip.

Male: rich red head and neck with a black breast and tail, gray sides, smoky gray wings and back, tricolored bill with a light blue base, white ring and black tip

Juvenile: similar to female

Nest: cup; female builds; 1 brood per year

Eggs: 9-14; pale white without markings

Incubation: 24-28 days; female and male incubate

Fledging: 56-73 days; female shows the young what to eat

Migration: complete to non-migrator in California

Food: seeds, aquatic plants, insects

Compare: The female Northern Shoveler (pg. 217) is a lighter brown with an exceptionally large shovel-shaped bill.

Stan's Notes: A duck of permanent large bodies of water. Forages along the shoreline, feeding on seeds, aquatic plants and insects. Usually builds nest directly on surface of water, using large mats of vegetation. Female lays up to 75 percent of its eggs in the nests of other Redheads and several other duck species. Nests primarily in the Prairie Pothole region of the northern Great Plains. The overall populations seem to be increasing at about 2-3 percent each year. Winters throughout California where it can find water.

female

male pg. 67

COMMON GOLDENEYE
Bucephala clangula

Size: 18½-20" (47-50 cm)

Female: A brown and gray duck with a large dark brown head and gray body. White collar. Bright golden eyes. Yellow-tipped dark bill.

Male: mostly white duck with a black back and a large, puffy green head, large white spot in front of each bright golden eye, dark bill

Juvenile: same as female, but has a dark bill

Nest: cavity; female lines old woodpecker cavity; 1 brood per year

Eggs: 8-10; light green without markings

Incubation: 28-32 days; female incubates

Fledging: 56-59 days; female leads young to food

Migration: complete, to California and Mexico

Food: aquatic plants, insects

Compare: Similar to, but larger than, the brown and white female Lesser Scaup (pg. 193). Look for female Goldeneye's dark brown head and white collar. Winter male and female Ruddy Duck (pg. 185) are smaller and lack yellow eyes.

Stan's Notes: Known for its loud whistling, produced by its wings in flight. In late winter and early spring, male often attracts female through elaborate displays, throwing its head backward while it utters a single raspy note. Female will lay eggs in other goldeneye nests, which results in some mothers incubating up to 30 eggs. Received the common name from its obvious bright golden eyes. Winters in California where it finds open water.

male pg. 337

female

MALLARD
Anas platyrhynchos

YEAR-ROUND

Size:	19-21" (48-53 cm)
Female:	All brown with orange and black bill. Small blue and white wing mark (speculum).
Male:	large, bulbous green head, white necklace, rust brown or chestnut chest, combination of gray and white on the sides, yellow bill, orange legs and feet
Juvenile:	same as female, but with a yellow bill
Nest:	ground; female builds; 1 brood per year
Eggs:	7-10; greenish to whitish, unmarked
Incubation:	26-30 days; female incubates
Fledging:	42-52 days; female leads young to food
Migration:	non-migrator to partial in California
Food:	seeds, plants, aquatic insects; will come to ground feeders offering corn
Compare:	Female Gadwall (pg. 213) has a gray bill with orange sides. Female Northern Pintail (pg. 215) is similar to female Mallard, but it has a gray bill. Female Northern Shoveler (pg. 217) has a spoon-shaped bill. Female Wood Duck (pg. 205) has a white eye-ring.

Stan's Notes: A familiar duck of lakes and ponds, it's considered a type of dabbling duck, tipping forward in shallow water to feed on aquatic plants on the bottom. The name "Mallard" comes from the Latin *masculus*, meaning "male," referring to the habit of males not taking part in raising ducklings. Both female and male have white tails and white underwings. Black central tail feathers of male curl upward. Will return to place of birth.

female

male pg. 313

GADWALL
Anas strepera

Size: 20" (50 cm)

Female: Very similar to the female Mallard. Mottled brown with pronounced color change from dark brown body to light brown neck and head. Wing linings are bright white, seen in flight. Small white wing patch, seen when swimming. Gray bill with orange sides.

Male: plump gray duck with a brown head and distinctive black rump, white belly, bright white wing linings, small white wing patch, chestnut-tinged wings, gray bill

Juvenile: similar to female

Nest: ground; female lines the nest with fine grass and down feathers plucked from her chest; 1 brood per year

Eggs: 8-11; white without markings

Incubation: 24-27 days; female incubates

Fledging: 48-56 days; young feed themselves

Migration: complete to non-migrator in California

Food: aquatic insects

Compare: The female Gadwall is very similar to female Mallard (pg. 211). Look for Gadwall's white wing patch and gray bill with orange sides.

Stan's Notes: A duck of shallow marshes. Consumes mostly plant material, dunking its head in water to feed rather than tipping forward, like other dabbling ducks. Walks well on land; feeds in fields and woodlands. Nests within 300 feet (100 m) of water. Often in pairs with other duck species. Establishes pair bond during winter.

male

female

YEAR-ROUND
WINTER

NORTHERN PINTAIL
Anas acuta

Size: 20" (50 cm), female
25" (63 cm), male

Male: A slender, elegant duck with a brown head, white neck, gray body and extremely long, narrow black tail. Gray bill. Non-breeding has a pale brown head that lacks the clear demarcation between the brown head and white neck. Lacks long tail feathers.

Female: mottled brown body with a paler head and neck, long tail, gray bill

Juvenile: similar to female

Nest: ground; female builds; 1 brood per year

Eggs: 6-9; olive green without markings

Incubation: 22-25 days; female incubates

Fledging: 36-50 days; female teaches young to feed

Migration: non-migrator to partial in California

Food: aquatic plants and insects, seeds

Compare: The male Northern Pintail has a distinctive brown head and white neck. Look for the unique long tail feathers. The female Pintail is similar to female Mallard (pg. 211), but Mallard has an orange bill with black spots.

Stan's Notes: A common dabbling duck of marshes in California. Approximately 90 percent of its diet is aquatic plants from fresh water, except when the females feed heavily on aquatic insects prior to nesting, presumably to gain extra nutrients for egg production. Male holds tail upright from the water's surface. No other North American duck has such a long tail.

male pg. 339

female

NORTHERN SHOVELER
Anas clypeata

MIGRATION
WINTER

Size: 20" (50 cm)

Female: Medium-sized brown duck speckled with black. Green speculum. An extraordinarily large spoon-shaped bill, almost always held pointed toward the water.

Male: same spoon-shaped bill, iridescent green head, rusty sides and white breast

Juvenile: same as female

Nest: ground; female builds; 1 brood per year

Eggs: 9-12; olive without markings

Incubation: 22-25 days; female incubates

Fledging: 30-60 days; female leads young to food

Migration: complete, to California, Mexico and Central America

Food: aquatic insects, plants

Compare: Similar color as female Mallard (pg. 211), but Mallard lacks the Shoveler's large bill. Female Redhead (pg. 207) is overall lighter brown and has a dark gray bill with a black tip. Look for Shoveler's large spoon-shaped bill to help identify.

Stan's Notes: One of several species of shoveler, so called because of the peculiar shape of its bill. The Northern Shoveler is the only species of these ducks in North America. Found in small flocks of 5-10, swimming low in water with its large bill pointed toward the water, as if it's too heavy to lift. Feeds mainly by filtering tiny aquatic insects and plants from the water's surface with its bill. Winters in California where it can find water.

male pg. 311

female

NORTHERN HARRIER
Circus cyaneus

YEAR-ROUND
WINTER

Size: 20" (50 cm); up to 3½-foot wingspan

Female: A slim, low-flying hawk. Dark brown back with brown-streaked breast and belly. Large white rump patch and narrow black bands across tail. Tips of wings black. Yellow eyes.

Male: silver gray with large white rump patch and white belly, faint narrow bands across tail, tips of wings black, yellow eyes

Juvenile: similar to female, with an orange breast

Nest: platform, often on ground; female and male build; 1 brood per year

Eggs: 4-8; bluish white without markings

Incubation: 31-32 days; female incubates

Fledging: 30-35 days; male and female feed young

Migration: non-migrator to partial in California

Food: mice, snakes, insects, small birds

Compare: Slimmer than Red-tailed Hawk (pg. 221). Look for black bands on tail and a white rump patch.

Stan's Notes: One of the easiest hawks to identify. Harriers glide just above ground, following contours of the land while searching for prey. Holds its wings just above the horizontal position, tilting back and forth in the wind, similar to Turkey Vultures. Formerly called Marsh Hawk due to its habit of hunting over marshes. Feeds on the ground. Will perch on the ground to preen and rest. At any age, has a distinctive owl-like face disk.

soaring

RED-TAILED HAWK
Buteo jamaicensis

YEAR-ROUND

Size: 19-23" (48-58 cm); up to 4-foot wingspan

Male: Large hawk with amazing variety of colors from bird to bird, from chocolate brown to nearly all white. Usually a white breast and a distinctive brown belly band. Rust red tail, usually seen only from above. Underside of wing is white with a small dark patch on the leading edge near shoulder.

Female: same as male, only slightly larger

Juvenile: similar to adults, lacking the red tail, has a speckled chest and light eyes

Nest: platform; male and female build; 1 brood per year

Eggs: 2-3; white without markings or sometimes marked with brown

Incubation: 30-35 days; female and male incubate

Fledging: 45-46 days; male and female feed young

Migration: non-migrator to partial migrator

Food: mice, birds, snakes, insects, mammals

Compare: Red-shouldered Hawk (pg. 195) is much smaller and lacks a red tail and white chest.

Stan's Notes: A common hawk of open country and in cities in the state, frequently seen perching on freeway light posts, fences and trees. Look for it circling over open fields and roadsides, searching for prey. Their large stick nests are commonly seen in large trees along roads. Nests are lined with finer material such as evergreen tree needles. Will return to the same nest site each year. Develops red tail in the second year.

GREATER ROADRUNNER
Geococcyx californianus

YEAR-ROUND

Size: 23" (58 cm)

Male: Overall brown with white streaking. Has a conspicuous crest that can be raised and lowered. An extremely long tail and a long, pointed brown bill. Blue patch just behind eyes. Short round wings are darker brown than body. Long gray legs with large feet.

Female: same as male

Juvenile: similar to adult

Nest: platform, low in a tree, shrub or cactus; the female and male build; 1-2 broods per year

Eggs: 4-6; white without markings

Incubation: 18-20 days; male and female incubate

Fledging: 16-18 days; male and female feed young

Migration: non-migrator

Food: insects, reptiles, small mammals and birds

Compare: This uniquely shaped ground dweller with an extremely long tail and prominent crest is hard to confuse with other birds.

Stan's Notes: Cuckoo family member known for running quickly across the ground to catch prey. A formidable predator, can run up to 15 miles (24 km) per hour. Flies short distances, usually in a low glide after a running takeoff. Raises its tail high, lowers it slowly. A slow, descending, low-pitched "coo-coo-coo-coo." Males do most incubating and feeding of the young. Performs a distraction display to protect nest. Young can catch prey four weeks after leaving nest.

LONG-BILLED CURLEW
Numenius americanus

MIGRATION
SUMMER
WINTER

Size: 23" (58 cm), including bill

Male: Cinnamon brown with an extremely long, down-curved bill. Long bluish legs. Darker cinnamon wing linings, seen in flight.

Female: same as male, but with a longer bill

Juvenile: same as adults, but with a shorter bill

Nest: ground; female builds; 1 brood per year

Eggs: 5-7; olive green with brown markings

Incubation: 27-30 days; female and male incubate, the female during day, male at night

Fledging: 32-45 days; female and male feed young

Migration: complete, to parts of California, the coast of Mexico and Central and South America

Food: insects, worms, crabs, eggs

Compare: Spotted Sandpiper (pg. 141) is smaller, less than half the size of the Long-billed Curlew. Hard to mistake the exceptionally long bill.

Stan's Notes: The largest of shorebirds, with an appropriate name. The extremely long bill is greater than half the length of its body. Female has a longer bill than male. Juvenile has a short bill, which grows into a long bill during the first six months. Uses bill to probe deep into mud for insects and worms. Female incubates during the day, male during the night. Although a shorebird, it is often in grass fields away from the shore. Breeds in open valleys and flatlands. Will fly up to 6 miles (10 km) from nest site to find food. Does not nest in most of California, nesting in other western states such as Utah, Idaho, Wyoming and Montana. Spends the winter along the California coast and Mexico.

breeding

winter

WHITE-FACED IBIS
Plegadis chihi

YEAR-ROUND
MIGRATION
SUMMER

Size: 23" (58 cm)

Male: Appears brown with rusty red (chestnut) on upper body. Glossy brown with green sheen on lower body. Long, down-curved gray bill. White border on a light red face. Orange-red legs and feet. Deep red eyes. Winter has less chestnut and a pink mask and legs.

Female: same as male

Juvenile: similar to winter adult

Nest: platform, on ground, low in shrub or small tree; female and male build; 1 brood a year

Eggs: 2-4; blue or green with brown markings

Incubation: 21-23 days; female and male incubate

Fledging: 30-35 days; female and male feed young

Migration: complete, to southern California, Mexico

Food: insects, crayfish, frogs, small fish, shellfish

Compare: Black Oystercatcher (pg. 23) has a red bill and yellow legs. Avocet (pg. 65) is mostly black and white with an upturned bill.

Stan's Notes: Of the three ibis species in the U.S., this is the only one regularly seen in California. Usually in marshes and estuaries. When close by and in good light, appears glossy red with green, blue and purple highlights. Uses its long bill to find and eat aquatic insects and fish. Large groups fly in a straight line. Rapid, shallow wing beat, then a short glide. Nests near water in large colonies with egrets and herons. Builds a loose nest of thin twigs, leaves and roots, lined with green leaves. Male spends more time feeding young than the female. Common name comes from the white outline on face.

male pg. 341

female

RED-BREASTED MERGANSER
Mergus serrator

MIGRATION
WINTER

Size: 23" (58 cm)

Female: Overall brown-to-gray duck with a shaggy reddish head and crest. Long orange bill.

Male: shaggy green head and crest, a prominent white collar, rusty breast, black and white body, long orange bill

Juvenile: similar to female

Nest: ground; female builds; 1 brood per year

Eggs: 5-10; olive green without markings

Incubation: 29-30 days; female incubates

Fledging: 55-65 days; female feeds young

Migration: complete, to coastal California, Mexico and Central America

Food: fish, aquatic insects

Compare: Very similar to, but larger than, the female Hooded Merganser (pg. 199), which has a smaller, darker bill than the bill of female Red-breasted Merganser.

Stan's Notes: A very fast flier, clocked at up to 100 miles (161 km) per hour. Often seen flying low across the water. Needs a long take-off run with wings flapping to get airborne. Serrated bill helps it catch slippery fish. Usually a silent duck. Male sometimes gives a soft, catlike meow. Female gives a harsh "krrr-croak." Doesn't breed before 2 years of age. Male abandons female just after eggs are laid. Females often share a nest. Breeds in Alaska and northern Canada. Young leave the nest within 24 hours of hatching, never to return.

GREAT HORNED OWL
Bubo virginianus

Size: 21-25" (53-63 cm); up to 3½-foot wingspan

Male: Robust brown "horned" owl. Bright yellow eyes and V-shaped white throat resembling a necklace. Horizontal barring on the chest.

Female: same as male, only slightly larger

Juvenile: similar to adults, lacking ear tufts

Nest: no nest; takes over the nests of crows, Great Blue Herons and hawks, or will use partial cavities, stumps or broken-off trees; 1 brood per year

Eggs: 2; white without markings

Incubation: 26-30 days; female incubates

Fledging: 30-35 days; male and female feed young

Migration: non-migrator

Food: mammals, birds (ducks), snakes, insects

Compare: Burrowing Owl (pg. 159) is much smaller, has long legs and lacks the Great Horned's feather tuft "horns." Over twice the size of its cousin, Western Screech-Owl (pg. 283).

Stan's Notes: One of the earliest nesting birds in the state, laying eggs in January and February. Has excellent hearing; able to hear a mouse moving beneath a foot of snow. "Ears" are actually tufts of feathers (horns) and have nothing to do with hearing. Not able to turn its head all the way around. Wing feathers are ragged on ends, resulting in a silent flight. The eyelids close from the top down, like humans. Fearless, it is one of the few animals that will kill skunks and porcupines. Because of this, it is sometimes called Flying Tiger.

male

female

RING-NECKED PHEASANT
Phasianus colchicus

YEAR-ROUND

Size: 30-36" (76-90 cm), male, including tail
21-25" (53-63 cm), female, including tail

Male: Golden brown body with a long tail. White ring around neck with purple, green, blue and red head.

Female: smaller, less flamboyant all-brown bird with a long tail

Juvenile: similar to female, with a shorter tail

Nest: ground; female builds; 1 brood per year

Eggs: 8-10; olive brown without markings

Incubation: 23-25 days; female incubates

Fledging: 11-12 days; female leads young to food

Migration: non-migrator

Food: insects, seeds, fruit; visits ground feeders

Compare: Much larger than California Quail (pg. 291) and lacks a teardrop plume on the forehead. The male Ring-necked is brightly colored.

Stan's Notes: Introduced to California from China during the late 1800s. Common now across the U.S. Like many other game birds, their numbers vary greatly, making them common in some years and scarce in others. "Ring-necked" refers to the thin white ring around the male's neck. "Pheasant" comes from the Greek word *phaisianos*, meaning "bird of the River Phasis." (The Phasis, located in Europe, is now known as the River Rioni.) Roosts on the ground or in trees at night. Listen for male's cackling call to attract females.

soaring

juvenile

GOLDEN EAGLE
Aquila chrysaetos

YEAR-ROUND
WINTER

Size: 30-40" (76-102 cm); up to 7-foot wingspan

Male: Uniform dark brown with golden head and nape of neck. Yellow around the base of bill and yellow feet.

Female: same as male

Juvenile: similar to adult, but has white wrist patches and white base of tail

Nest: platform, on cliff; female and male build; 1 brood per year

Eggs: 2; white with brown markings

Incubation: 43-45 days; female and male incubate

Fledging: 66-75 days; female and male feed young

Migration: non-migrator to partial migrator; will move around to find food

Food: mammals, birds, reptiles, insects

Compare: Similar to Bald Eagle (pg. 75), lacking the white head and tail. Juvenile Golden Eagle, with its white wrist marks and base of tail, is often confused with juvenile Bald Eagle.

Stan's Notes: Large and powerful bird of prey that has no trouble taking larger prey such as jack rabbits. Hunts by perching or soaring and watching for movement. Inhabits mountainous terrain, requiring large territories to provide large supply of food. Thought to mate for life, renewing pair bond late in winter with spectacular high-flying courtship displays. Usually nests on cliff faces, rarely in trees. Uses well-established nest that has been used for generations. Not uncommon for it to add things to nest such as antlers, bones and barbed wire.

WILD TURKEY
Meleagris gallopavo

YEAR-ROUND

Size: 36-48" (90-120 cm)

Male: Large, plump brown and bronze bird with striking blue and red bare head. Fan tail and long, straight black beard in center of chest. Spurs on legs.

Female: thinner and less striking than male, usually lacking breast beard

Juvenile: same as adult of the same sex

Nest: ground; female builds; 1 brood per year

Eggs: 10-12; buff white with dull brown markings

Incubation: 27-28 days; female incubates

Fledging: 6-10 days; female leads young to food

Migration: non-migrator

Food: insects, seeds, fruit

Compare: This bird is quite distinctive and unlikely to be confused with others.

Stan's Notes: The largest game bird in the state, and the bird from which the domestic turkey was bred. Almost became our national bird, losing to the Bald Eagle by a single vote. A strong flier that can approach 60 miles (97 km) per hour. Able to fly straight up, then away. Eyesight is three times better than human eyesight. Hearing is also excellent; can hear competing males up to a mile away. Males hold "harems" of up to 20 females. Males are called toms, females are hens and young are poults. Roosts in trees at night.

in flight

non-breeding

breeding

juvenile

BROWN PELICAN
Pelecanus occidentalis

Size: 48" (120 cm); up to 9-foot wingspan

Male: Brown gray body with a black belly and an exceptionally long bill. Breeding has a white or yellow head, dark chestnut hind neck and a bright red expandable throat pouch. Non-breeding has a white head and neck and a gray throat pouch.

Female: similar to male

Juvenile: brown with white breast and belly, does not acquire adult plumage until third year

Nest: platform; female and male build; 1 brood per year

Eggs: 2-4; white without markings

Incubation: 28-30 days; female and male incubate

Fledging: 71-86 days; female and male feed young

Migration: complete to non-migrator along the coast of California

Food: fish

Compare: An unmistakable bird in California.

Stan's Notes: A coastal bird of California. Recently an endangered species, it is reestablishing along the West, East and Gulf coasts after populations suffered from eggshell thinning during the 1970s due to DDT and other pesticides. Captures fish by diving headfirst into the ocean, opening its large bill and "netting" fish with its gular pouch. Frequently seen sitting on posts at marinas. Nests in large colonies. Doesn't breed before age 3, when it obtains its breeding plumage. The Pacific variety (shown) has a bright red throat pouch unlike the brown throat patch of Gulf coast and Atlantic pelicans.

RUBY-CROWNED KINGLET
Regulus calendula

SUMMER
WINTER

Size: 4" (10 cm)

Male: Small, teardrop-shaped green-to-gray bird with 2 white wing bars and a hidden ruby crown. White eye-ring.

Female: same as male, but lacking the ruby crown

Juvenile: same as female

Nest: pendulous; female builds; 1 brood per year

Eggs: 4-5; white with brown markings

Incubation: 11-12 days; female incubates

Fledging: 11-12 days; female and male feed young

Migration: complete, to most of California, Mexico

Food: insects, berries

Compare: The female American Goldfinch (pg. 387) is larger, but shares the same olive color and unmarked breast. Look for the white eye-ring of Ruby-crowned Kinglet.

Stan's Notes: One of the smaller birds in the state. It takes a quick eye to see the male's ruby crown. Most commonly seen during the spring and fall migrations, when groups travel together. Look for it flitting around thick shrubs low to the ground. Female builds an unusual pendulous (sac-like) nest, intricately woven and decorated on the outside with colored lichens and mosses stuck together with spider webs. The nest is suspended from a branch overlapped by leaves and usually is hung high in a mature tree. The common name "Kinglet" comes from the Anglo-Saxon word *cyning*, or "king," referring to the male's ruby crown, and the diminutive suffix "let," meaning "small." A winter resident in most of California.

PYGMY NUTHATCH
Sitta pygmaea

YEAR-ROUND

Size: 4¼" (10.5 cm)

Male: Tiny gray-blue black bird with gray-brown crown. Creamy chest with a lighter chin. A relatively short tail, large head and long bill.

Female: same as male

Juvenile: same as adult

Nest: cavity; female and male construct; 1 brood per year

Eggs: 4-8; white with brown markings

Incubation: 14-16 days; female incubates

Fledging: 20-22 days; female and male feed young

Migration: non-migrator

Food: insects, berries, seeds; will visit seed feeders

Compare: Smaller than the Red-breasted Nuthatch (pg. 245) and the White-breasted Nuthatch (pg. 253). The Red-breasted has a rusty red breast unlike the creamy breast of Pygmy. White-breasted has a distinctive black cap and a white chest.

Stan's Notes: A nuthatch of pine forests. Unlike the White-breasted Nuthatch, the Pygmy Nuthatch requires mature pines with old or decaying wood. Usually drills its own nest cavity. While it does not migrate, it forms winter flocks with chickadees and other birds and moves around to find food. Usually feeds in the crown of a tree or at the ends of twigs and branches, where it searches for insects and seeds. This is unlike White-breasted and Red-breasted Nuthatches, which usually search trunks of trees for food.

YEAR-ROUND
WINTER

RED-BREASTED NUTHATCH
Sitta canadensis

Size: 4½" (11 cm)

Male: A small gray-backed bird with a black cap and a prominent eye line. A rust red breast and belly.

Female: gray cap, pale undersides

Juvenile: same as female

Nest: cavity; female builds; 1 brood per year

Eggs: 5-6; white with red brown markings

Incubation: 11-12 days; female incubates

Fledging: 14-20 days; female and male feed young

Migration: non-migrator to irruptive migrator; moves around the state in search of food

Food: insects, seeds; visits seed and suet feeders

Compare: Slightly larger than the Pygmy Nuthatch (pg. 243) and smaller than White-breasted Nuthatch (pg. 253), neither of which has the rich red breast of the Red-breasted.

Stan's Notes: Red-breasted Nuthatch behaves like White-breasted and Pygmy Nuthatches, climbing down trunks of trees headfirst. Similar to chickadees, visits seed feeders, quickly grabbing a seed and flying off to crack it open. Will wedge a seed into a crevice and pound it open with several sharp blows. The name "Nuthatch" comes from the Middle English moniker *nuthak*, referring to the bird's habit of wedging a seed into a crevice and hacking it open. Look for it in mature conifers, frequently extracting seeds from cones. Doesn't excavate a cavity as the chickadee might; rather, it takes over a former woodpecker or chickadee cavity.

breeding

non-breeding

CALIFORNIA GNATCATCHER
Polioptila californica

YEAR-ROUND

Size: 4½" (11 cm)

Male: Gray with a black crown extending below the eyes. Long black tail with some white beneath. Non-breeding lacks a black crown and has a small black streak over each eye.

Female: similar to non-breeding male, lacks a black streak over each eye

Juvenile: similar to female

Nest: cup; female and male construct; 1-3 broods per year

Eggs: 3-5; pale blue with light brown markings

Incubation: 12-14 days; female and male incubate

Fledging: 10-15 days; female and male feed young

Migration: non-migrator

Food: insects

Compare: Blue-gray Gnatcatcher (pg. 79) is pale blue, has a white underside of tail and lacks the breeding male California's black crown.

Stan's Notes: In brush or coastal sage scrub in southern California and Mexico only. Avoids dense or tall stands of sage scrub. Prefers burned areas. Was listed as a federally threatened species in 1993 and species of special concern in California. Dwindling population due to coastal land development. Often in pairs. Feeds on insects on leaves of sagebrush and other plants. Home range of 5-10 acres (2-4 ha). Maintains territory all year. Builds its nest 3 feet (.9 m) off the ground, making it easy for predators to destroy. The lower the nest, the more likely it will be predated. A cowbird host. Some pairs abandon the nest when a cowbird egg is introduced.

BUSHTIT
Psaltriparus minimus

YEAR-ROUND

Size: 4½" (11 cm)

Male: A dull gray bird with a slightly brown cap. Relatively long tail. Black eyes and legs, and a tiny black bill.

Female: same as male, but has pale yellow eyes

Juvenile: similar to adults, with dark brown eyes

Nest: pendulous; female and male construct; 1-2 broods per year

Eggs: 5-7; white without markings

Incubation: 10-12 days; female and male incubate

Fledging: 14-15 days; female and male feed young

Migration: non-migrator

Food: insects, seeds, fruit; comes to seed feeders

Compare: Chestnut-backed (pg. 99) and Mountain (pg. 259) Chickadees are larger and have black crowns and white on their faces. Oak Titmouse (pg. 261) has a crest.

Stan's Notes: A lively bird, often seen in extended family flocks of up to 20 individuals in open woods and low woodlands. It is often seen with other bird species such as kinglets, wrens and chickadees. Easily picked out by its small size, long tail and the extremely short bill. Groups will roost together, huddling tightly to keep warm and save energy. Eyes are pale yellow in adult females, dark brown in juveniles and black in adult males. Away from the coast, adults lack the brown cap, appearing all dull gray.

male

female

juvenile

VERDIN
Auriparus flaviceps

YEAR-ROUND

Size: 4½" (11 cm)

Male: Light gray to silvery overall. Lemon yellow head. Rusty red shoulder patch, frequently hidden. Short, pointed dark bill. Dark mark between bill and eyes. Dark legs and feet.

Female: duller than male

Juvenile: overall gray, lacks the yellow head, dark bill and rusty red shoulder patch

Nest: covered cup; male builds; 1-2 broods a year

Eggs: 4-5; bluish green with brown markings

Incubation: 8-10 days; female incubates

Fledging: 19-21 days; female and male feed young

Migration: non-migrator

Food: seeds, insects, fruit, nectar; comes to nectar feeders and orange halves

Compare: Smaller than the Oak Titmouse (pg. 261), which has a crest and lacks a yellow head. The Mountain Chickadee (pg. 259) has an obvious black cap, chin and eye line.

Stan's Notes: A very friendly bird that can be a regular visitor to nectar feeders and orange halves. Often hides its rusty red shoulder marks, confusing the novice bird watcher. Most easily identified as a tiny gray bird with a yellow head. Male builds several ball-shaped, conspicuous nests of thorny twigs, interweaves them with leaves and grass and lines them with feathers and plant down. Male shows the nest possibilities to female and she selects one. After fledging, young return to nest at night unlike most small birds, which leave and don't return for shelter. Often uses nest for several seasons.

WHITE-BREASTED NUTHATCH
Sitta carolinensis

Size: 5-6" (13-15 cm)

Male: Slate gray with a white face and belly, and black cap and nape. Long thin bill, slightly upturned. Chestnut undertail.

Female: similar to male, gray cap and nape

Juvenile: similar to female

Nest: cavity; female and male construct; 1 brood per year

Eggs: 5-7; white with brown markings

Incubation: 11-12 days; female incubates

Fledging: 13-14 days; female and male feed young

Migration: non-migrator

Food: insects, seeds; visits seed and suet feeders

Compare: Red-breasted Nuthatch (pg. 245) is smaller with a rusty belly and distinctive black eye line. Pygmy Nuthatch (pg. 243) lacks the White-breasted's black cap. The California Gnatcatcher (pg. 247) lacks a white face.

Stan's Notes: The nuthatch's habit of hopping headfirst down tree trunks helps it see insects and insect eggs that birds climbing up the trunk might miss. Incredible climbing agility comes from an extra-long hind toe claw or nail, nearly twice the size of the front toe claws. The name "Nuthatch" comes from the Middle English moniker *nuthak*, referring to the bird's habit of wedging a seed into a crevice and hacking it open. Often seen in flocks with chickadees. Mated pairs will stay together all year, defending small territories. Listen for its characteristic spring call, "whi-whi-whi-whi," given in February and March. One of 17 worldwide nuthatch species.

male

female

YEAR-ROUND
WINTER

YELLOW-RUMPED WARBLER
Dendroica coronata

Size: 5-6" (13-15 cm)

Male: Slate gray bird with a black chest and streaks on flanks. Yellow patch on rump, head and flanks. Yellow chin. White belly. Single large white wing bar.

Female: duller than male, lacks the black chest, has the same yellow patches

Juvenile: light brown version of female

Nest: cup; female builds; 2 broods per year

Eggs: 4-5; white with brown markings

Incubation: 12-13 days; female incubates

Fledging: 10-12 days; female and male feed young

Migration: partial to non-migrator in California

Food: insects, berries; rarely comes to suet feeders

Compare: Male Wilson's Warbler (pg. 381) has a black cap. Male Yellow Warbler (pg. 393) is yellow with orange streaks on breast. Yellowthroat (pg. 389) has a yellow chest and black mask. Look for yellow patches on Yellow-rumped's rump, head, chin and flanks to help identify.

Stan's Notes: A common warbler in California. Nests in coniferous and aspen forests. Flocks of hundreds are seen when northern birds join residents for winter. Usually arrives in late September to early October. Frequently called Audubon's Warbler in western states and Myrtle Warbler in eastern states. Sometimes called Butter-butts due to the yellow patch on rump. Familiar call is a single, robust "chip," heard mostly during winter. Also has a wonderful song in spring.

female
pg. 111

male

Oregon male

DARK-EYED JUNCO
Junco hyemalis

YEAR-ROUND WINTER

Size: 5½" (14 cm)

Male: A round, dark-eyed bird with slate-gray-to-charcoal chest, head and back. White belly. Pink bill. Since the outermost tail feathers are white, tail appears as a white V in flight.

Female: same as male, only tan-to-brown color

Juvenile: similar to female, but has a streaked breast and head

Nest: cup; female and male build; 2 broods a year

Eggs: 3-5; white with reddish brown markings

Incubation: 12-13 days; female incubates

Fledging: 10-13 days; male and female feed young

Migration: partial to non-migrator in California

Food: seeds, insects; will come to seed feeders

Compare: Rarely confused with any other bird. Small flocks feed under bird feeders in winter.

Stan's Notes: Several junco species have now been combined into one, simply called Dark-eyed Junco (see lower inset). It is one of the most numerous wintering birds in the state. A common year-round resident in parts of California. Spends the winter in the foothills and plains after snowmelt and returns to higher elevations to nest. Nests in a wide variety of wooded habitats during April and May. Adheres to a rigid social hierarchy, with the dominant birds chasing the less dominant birds. Look for its white outer tail feathers flashing when in flight. Most comfortable on the ground, juncos "double-scratch" with both feet to expose seeds and insects. Eats many weed seeds. Usually seen on the ground in small flocks.

MOUNTAIN CHICKADEE
Poecile gambeli

YEAR-ROUND

Size: 5½" (14 cm)

Male: Overall gray with a black cap, chin and line through the eyes. White eyebrows.

Female: same as male

Juvenile: similar to adult

Nest: cavity, old woodpecker hole or excavates its own; female and male build; 1-2 broods per year

Eggs: 5-8; white without markings

Incubation: 11-14 days; female and male incubate

Fledging: 18-21 days; female and male feed young

Migration: non-migrator to partial migrator

Food: seeds, insects; visits seed and suet feeders

Compare: Larger than Bushtit (pg. 249), which lacks the black cap and white on the face. Oak Titmouse (pg. 261) is larger and has a crest. The Verdin (pg. 251) is smaller and has a yellow head.

Stan's Notes: An abundant bird in the state, but more common in coniferous forests in mountainous regions of California. Prefers old growth spruce, fir and pine forests. Feeds heavily on coniferous seeds and insects. Flocks with other birds during winter. Moves to lower elevations in winter, returning to high elevations for nesting. Excavates a nest cavity or uses an old woodpecker hole. Will use a nest box. Occasionally uses the same nest site year after year. Lines its nest with moss, hair and feathers. Female will not leave her nest if disturbed, but will hiss and flutter wings.

OAK TITMOUSE
Baeolophus inornatus

YEAR-ROUND

Size: 6" (15 cm)

Male: Overall gray with brown tinges. Short crest. Small gray bill. Dark eyes.

Female: same as male

Juvenile: similar to adult, with a shorter crest

Nest: cavity; female and male line the cavity; 1-2 broods per year

Eggs: 3-6; pale white without markings

Incubation: 14-16 days; female incubates

Fledging: 18-21 days; female and male feed young

Migration: non-migrator

Food: insects, seeds, fruit; comes to seed feeders

Compare: Larger than Bushtit (pg. 249), which lacks the crest. Larger than Mountain Chickadee (pg. 259), which has a black cap, chin and line through its eyes.

Stan's Notes: Until recently, Oak Titmouse and Juniper Titmouse (not shown) were one species, called Plain Titmouse. The Oak Titmouse is seen only in California. Juniper is in many Southwest states. Seen in dry, open oak woodlands, hence its common name. Often heard before seen. A loud repeated whistle, "teewee-teewee-teewee." A very active species and an acrobat, sometimes hanging upside down from tree limbs, searching for insects. Constructs nest of moss, feathers and fur inside an old woodpecker hole or a nest box, when available. Will use a roosting box at night for protection against the cold and predators. Pairs usually stay together through the year. Often seen in mixed flocks of birds during winter. Male feeds the female in spring to reestablish the pair bond.

BLACK-THROATED SPARROW
Amphispiza bilineata

YEAR-ROUND
SUMMER

Size: 6" (15 cm)

Male: Overall smooth gray bird with bold black and white markings on head and face, and large black patch on the throat. Darker gray tail with white edges.

Female: same as male

Juvenile: similar to adult, lacks the black and white head pattern and black throat

Nest: cup; female builds; 1-2 broods per year

Eggs: 3-4; pale blue to white without markings

Incubation: 12-14 days; female incubates

Fledging: 10-12 days; female and male feed young

Migration: complete, to southeastern California, Mexico

Food: insects, seeds, leaf buds

Compare: White-crowned Sparrow (pg. 127) shares the bold black and white coloring on head, but lacks the large black throat patch. Look for a black patch on the throat of a smooth gray sparrow to identify.

Stan's Notes: A sparrow of desert scrub and rocky uplands. Male often perches on prominent spots in its territory and sings a short, simple, tinkling song or a high, bell-like "tee-tee-tee." Often holds off breeding until rainfall produces enough food. Female constructs a cup nest of dried grass low in a cactus and lines it with finer plant materials. Although the young are fed a diet of insects, adults will eat new green shoots of trees, shrubs and grasses along with insects and seeds. Forms small flocks in the winter of up to 20 individuals, often with other sparrow species.

male pg. 357

female

VERMILION FLYCATCHER
Pyrocephalus rubinus

YEAR-ROUND
SUMMER

Size: 6" (15 cm)

Female: A mostly gray bird with a gray head, neck and back. Nearly white chin and chest. Pink belly to undertail. Black tail. Thin black bill.

Male: crimson red head, crest, chin, breast and belly, black nape of neck, back, wings and tail, black line through eyes, thin black bill

Juvenile: similar to female, lacks a pink undertail

Nest: cup; female builds; 1-2 broods per year

Eggs: 2-4; white with brown markings

Incubation: 14-16 days; female and male incubate

Fledging: 14-16 days; female and male feed young

Migration: complete migrator to non-migrator in parts of southern California

Food: insects (mainly bees)

Compare: Similar body and bill shape as the phoebes of California and similar habitat. The Say's Phoebe (pg. 271) has a pale orange belly. The Black Phoebe (pg. 37) is nearly all black with a white belly.

Stan's Notes: Frequently seen in open areas with shrubs and small trees close to water. Will perch on a thin branch, pumping its tail up and down while waiting for an aerial insect. Flies out to snatch it up, then returns to perch. Will drop to the ground for terrestrial insects. Male raises its crest, fluffs chest feathers, fans tail and sings a song during a fluttery flight to court females. Female constructs a shallow cup nest of twigs and grasses and lines it with downy plant material. Male feeds female during incubation and brooding.

breeding
pg. 121

winter

LEAST SANDPIPER
Calidris minutilla

MIGRATION
WINTER

Size: 6" (15 cm)

Male: Overall gray to light brown winter plumage with a distinct brown breast band and light gray eyebrows. White belly and dull yellow legs. Short, down-curved black bill.

Female: same as male

Juvenile: similar to winter adult, but buff brown and lacking the breast band

Nest: ground; male and female construct; 1 brood per year

Eggs: 3-4; olive with dark markings

Incubation: 19-23 days; male and female incubate

Fledging: 25-28 days; male and female feed young

Migration: complete, to parts of California, Mexico and Central America

Food: aquatic and terrestrial insects, seeds

Compare: The smallest of sandpipers. Often confused with winter Western Sandpiper (pg. 269). Least Sandpiper's yellow legs differentiate it from other tiny sandpipers. The short, thin, down-curved bill also helps to identify.

Stan's Notes: A winter resident in parts of California. The smallest of peeps (sandpipers) that nest on the tundra in northern regions of Canada and Alaska. Yellow legs can be hard to see in water, poor light or when covered with mud. Prefers grassy flats of saltwater and freshwater ponds. A tame sandpiper that can be approached without scaring.

breeding
pg. 123

winter

WESTERN SANDPIPER
Calidris mauri

MIGRATION
WINTER

Size: 6½" (16 cm)

Male: Winter plumage is dull gray to light brown overall with a white belly and eyebrows. Black legs. Narrow bill that droops near tip.

Female: same as male

Juvenile: similar to breeding adult, bright buff brown on back only

Nest: ground; male and female construct; 1 brood per year

Eggs: 2-4; light brown with dark markings

Incubation: 20-22 days; male and female incubate

Fledging: 19-21 days; male and female feed young

Migration: complete, to coastal California, Mexico and Central America

Food: aquatic and terrestrial insects

Compare: Very often confused with the winter Least Sandpiper (pg. 267). Look for black legs to differentiate from Least Sandpiper. Western has a longer bill that droops slightly at tip.

Stan's Notes: A winter resident along coastal California and long-distance migrant. Nests on the ground in large "loose" colonies on the tundra of northern coastal Alaska. Adults leave their breeding grounds several weeks before young. Some obtain their breeding plumage before leaving California in spring. Feeds on insects at the water's edge, sometimes immersing its head. Young leave the nest (precocial) within a few hours after hatching. Female leaves and the male tends the hatchlings.

SAY'S PHOEBE
Sayornis saya

YEAR-ROUND
MIGRATION
SUMMER
WINTER

Size: 7½" (19 cm)

Male: Overall dark gray, darkest on head, tail and wings. Belly and undertail tawny. Black bill.

Female: same as male

Juvenile: similar to adult, but browner overall with 2 tawny wing bars and a yellow lower bill

Nest: cup; female builds; 1-2 broods per year

Eggs: 3-6; pale white with brown markings

Incubation: 12-14 days; female incubates

Fledging: 14-16 days; female and male feed young

Migration: complete to partial migrator, to coastal and southern California, Mexico, Central and South America

Food: insects, berries

Compare: Female Vermilion Flycatcher (pg. 265) is smaller and has a pink belly.

Stan's Notes: Widespread throughout California below 9,000-foot (2,750 m) elevations. Nests in cliff crevices, abandoned buildings, bridges and other vertical structures. Frequently uses the same nest several times in a season, returning the following year to that same nest. Has a nearly all-insect diet. Flies out from a perch to grab an aerial insect and returns to the same perch (hawking). Also hunts insects on the ground, hovering and dropping down to catch them. Phoebes are classified as New World Flycatchers and aren't related to Old World Flycatchers. Named after Thomas Say, who is said to have discovered this bird in Colorado. The genus, species and first part of its common name refer to Mr. Say. Common name "Phoebe" is likely an imitation of the bird's call.

AMERICAN DIPPER
Cinclus mexicanus

YEAR-ROUND

Size: 7½" (19 cm)

Male: Dark gray to black overall. Head is slightly lighter in color. A short upturned tail. Dark eyes and bill.

Female: same as male

Juvenile: similar to adult, only paler with white eyelids that are most noticeable when blinking

Nest: pendulous, covered nest with the entrance near the bottom, on cliff, behind waterfall; female builds; 1-2 broods per year

Eggs: 3-5; white without markings

Incubation: 13-17 days; female incubates

Fledging: 18-25 days; female and male feed young

Migration: non-migrator; seeks moving open water

Food: aquatic insects, small fish, crustaceans

Compare: Similar shape as American Robin (pg. 287), but lacks a red breast. The only songbird in the state that dives into fast-moving water.

Stan's Notes: A common bird of fast, usually noisy streams that provide some kind of protected shelf on which to construct a nest. Some have had success attracting with man-made ledges. Plunges headfirst into fast-moving water, looking for just about any aquatic insect, propelling itself underwater with its wings. Frequently seen emerging with a large insect, which it smashes against rock before eating. Has the ability to fly directly into the air from underwater. Depending on snowmelt, nesting usually starts in March or April. Dippers in lower elevations often nest a second time each season.

winter

breeding
pg. 143

SANDERLING
Calidris alba

WINTER

Size: 8" (20 cm)

Male: The lightest sandpiper on the beach during winter. Winter plumage head and back are gray and belly is white. Black legs and bill. White wing stripe, seen only in flight.

Female: same as male

Juvenile: spotty black on the head and back, a white belly, black legs and bill

Nest: ground; male builds; 1-2 broods per year

Eggs: 3-4; greenish olive with brown markings

Incubation: 24-30 days; male and female incubate

Fledging: 16-17 days; female and male feed young

Migration: complete, to coastal California, Mexico and Central and South America

Food: insects

Compare: Same size as the winter plumage Spotted Sandpiper (pg. 141). Similar color as the winter Black-bellied Plover (pg. 295), but much smaller with a smaller bill.

Stan's Notes: One of the most common shorebirds in the state, but mostly seen in gray winter plumage from August to April. Can be seen in groups on sandy beaches, running out with each retreating wave to feed. Look for a flash of white on wings when it is in flight. Occasionally the female will mate with several males (polyandry), resulting in males and the female incubating separate nests. Both sexes will perform a distraction display if threatened. Nests on the Arctic tundra.

female

male pg. 7

PHAINOPEPLA
Phainopepla nitens

YEAR-ROUND
SUMMER

Size: 8" (20 cm)

Female: Slim, long, mostly gray bird with a ragged crest and deep red eyes. Whitish wing bars.

Male: slim, long, glossy black bird with a ragged crest and deep red eyes, wing patches near tips of wings are white, obvious in flight

Juvenile: similar to female

Nest: cup; female and male construct; 1-2 broods per year

Eggs: 2-4; gray with brown markings

Incubation: 12-14 days; female and male incubate

Fledging: 18-20 days; female and male feed young

Migration: complete, to California and Arizona

Food: fruit (usually mistletoe), insects; will come to water elements or water drips in yards

Compare: Clark's Nutcracker (pg. 297) is similar, but lacks a crest.

Stan's Notes: Seen in desert scrub with water and mistletoe nearby. Gives a low, liquid "kweer" song, but will also mimic other species. In winter individuals defend food supply such as a single tree with abundant mistletoe berries. Probably responsible for the dispersal of mistletoe plants far and wide. Male will fly up to a height of 300 feet (90 m), circling and zigzagging to court female. Builds nest of twigs and plant fibers and binds it with spider webs in the crotch of a mistletoe cluster. Lines nest with hair or soft plant fibers. May be the only species to nest in two regions in the same nest season. Nests in dry desert habitat in early spring. When it gets hot, moves to a higher area with an abundant water supply to nest again.

TOWNSEND'S SOLITAIRE
Myadestes townsendi

YEAR-ROUND WINTER

Size: 8½" (22 cm)

Male: All-gray robin look-alike with a prominent white ring around each eye. Wings slightly darker than the body. Long tail. Short dark bill and dark legs.

Female: same as male

Juvenile: darker gray with a tan scaly appearance

Nest: cup; female builds; 1-2 broods per year

Eggs: 3-5; blue, green, gray or white with brown markings

Incubation: 12-14 days; female incubates

Fledging: 10-14 days; female and male feed young

Migration: non-migrator to partial in parts of California; known to migrate to eastern states

Food: insects, fruit

Compare: American Robin (pg. 287) has a red breast. The Clark's Nutcracker (pg. 297) has black wings. Northern Mockingbird (pg. 289) lacks the white eye-ring.

Stan's Notes: A summer resident of coniferous mountain forests, moving lower in winter. "Hawks" for insects, perching in trees and darting out to capture them. Eats berries in winter when insects are not available and actively defends a good berry source from other birds. Builds nest on ground sheltered by rocks or an overhang, or sometimes low in a tree or shrub. Song is a series of clear flute-like whistles without a distinct pattern. Shows white outer tail feathers and light tan patches on wings when in flight.

SAGE THRASHER
Oreoscoptes montanus

MIGRATION
SUMMER
WINTER

Size: 8½" (22 cm)

Male: Light gray overall with a heavily streaked white breast. Distinctive white chin. Yellow orange eyes. Darker gray tail with white tip.

Female: same as male

Juvenile: duller version of adult

Nest: cup; female and male construct; 1-2 broods per year

Eggs: 3-5; blue with brown markings

Incubation: 13-17 days; female and male incubate

Fledging: 11-14 days; female and male feed young

Migration: complete, to southern California, Mexico, Central America

Food: insects, fruit

Compare: The California Thrasher (pg. 169) is much larger and lacks a streaked breast and belly. Hermit Thrush (pg. 133) is darker brown. Cactus Wren (pg. 147) has a down-curved bill. Northern Mockingbird (pg. 289) has white wing patches, as seen in flight.

Stan's Notes: More common in the sagebrush regions of the state. Males are often seen and heard as they sing from the tops of shrubs. Constructs a large and bulky nest beneath or at the base of dense cover in an attempt to keep the nest shaded. Sometimes builds a twig platform over the nest if existing cover doesn't provide enough shade. Old nests are sometimes used by Gambel's Quails. Returns in April. Nests in May. Populations increasing in California over the past few decades.

gray morph

brown morph

WESTERN SCREECH-OWL
Megascops kennicottii

YEAR-ROUND

Size: 8½" (22 cm); up to 1½-foot wingspan

Male: A small, overall gray owl with bright yellow eyes. Two short ear tufts. A short tail. Some birds are brownish.

Female: same as male

Juvenile: similar to adult of the same morph, lacks ear tufts

Nest: cavity; uses old woodpecker hole; 1 brood per year

Eggs: 2-6; white without markings

Incubation: 21-30 days; female incubates

Fledging: 25-30 days; female and male feed young

Migration: non-migrator

Food: insects, small mammals, birds

Compare: Burrowing Owl (pg. 159) is slightly larger and lacks ear tufts. Western Screech-Owl is hard to confuse with its considerably larger cousin, the Great Horned Owl (pg. 231).

Stan's Notes: The most common small owl throughout California. An owl of suburban woodlands and backyards. Requires trees that are at least a foot in diameter for nesting and roosting, so it usually is found in towns or in trees that have been preserved. A secondary cavity nester, which means it nests in tree cavities created by other birds. Usually not found in elevations above 4,000 feet (1,200 m). Densities in lower areas are about 1 bird per square mile (2-3 birds per sq. km). Most screech-owls are gray; some are brown.

LOGGERHEAD SHRIKE
Lanius ludovicianus

YEAR-ROUND
MIGRATION

Size: 9" (22.5 cm)

Male: A gray head and back with black wings and mask across the eyes. A white chin, breast and belly. Black tail, legs and feet. Black bill with hooked tip. White wing patches, seen in flight.

Female: same as male

Juvenile: dull version of adult

Nest: cup; male and female construct; 1-2 broods per year

Eggs: 4-7; off-white with dark markings

Incubation: 16-17 days; female incubates

Fledging: 17-21 days; female and male feed young

Migration: non-migrator to partial in California

Food: insects, lizards, small mammals, frogs

Compare: The Northern Mockingbird (pg. 289) has a similar color pattern, but lacks the black mask. Shrike is stockier than Mockingbird and perches in more open places. Cedar Waxwing (pg. 137) has a black mask, but is brown, not gray and black like Shrike.

Stan's Notes: The Loggerhead is a songbird that acts like a bird of prey. Known for skewering prey on barbed wire fences, thorns and other sharp objects to store or hold still while tearing apart to eat, hence its other common name, Butcher Bird. Feet are too weak to hold the prey it eats. Breeding bird surveys indicate declining populations in the Great Plains due to pesticides killing its major food source–grasshoppers.

male

female

AMERICAN ROBIN
Turdus migratorius

YEAR-ROUND WINTER

Size: 9-11" (22.5-28 cm)

Male: A familiar gray bird with a rusty red breast, and nearly black head and tail. White chin with black streaks. White eye-ring.

Female: similar to male, but with a gray head and a duller breast

Juvenile: similar to female, but has a speckled breast and brown back

Nest: cup; female builds with help from the male; 2-3 broods per year

Eggs: 4-7; pale blue without markings

Incubation: 12-14 days; female incubates

Fledging: 14-16 days; female and male feed young

Migration: non-migrator to complete in California

Food: insects, fruit, berries, worms

Compare: Familiar bird to all.

Stan's Notes: Although a complete migrator in northern states, it is a year-round resident in much of California. Can be heard singing all night long during spring. Most people don't realize how easy it is to differentiate between male and female robins. Compare the male's dark, nearly black head and brick red breast with the female's gray head and dull red breast. Robins are not listening for worms when they cock their heads to one side. They are looking with eyes placed far back on the sides of their heads. Very territorial bird. Often seen fighting its own reflection in windows. Northern birds join resident birds in California during winter, increasing the population.

displaying

NORTHERN MOCKINGBIRD
Mimus polyglottos

YEAR-ROUND

Size: 10" (25 cm)

Male: Silvery gray head and back with light gray chest and belly. White wing patches, seen in flight or during display. Tail mostly black with white outer tail feathers. Black bill.

Female: same as male

Juvenile: dull gray, a heavily streaked chest, gray bill

Nest: cup; female and male build; 2 broods per year, sometimes more

Eggs: 3-5; blue green with brown markings

Incubation: 12-13 days; female incubates

Fledging: 11-13 days; female and male feed young

Migration: non-migrator in California

Food: insects, fruit

Compare: Loggerhead Shrike (pg. 285) has a similar color pattern, but is stockier, has a black mask and perches in more open places. Townsend's Solitaire (pg. 279) has a white eye-ring. Look for Mockingbird to spread its wings, flash its white wing patches and wag its tail from side to side.

Stan's Notes: Very animated. Performs an elaborate mating dance. Facing each other with heads and tails erect, pairs run toward each other, flashing white wing patches, and then retreat to cover nearby. Thought to flash wing patches to scare up insects when hunting. Sits for long periods of time on top of a shrub. Imitates other birds (vocal mimicry), hence the common name. Young males often sing at night. Often unafraid of people, allowing for close observation.

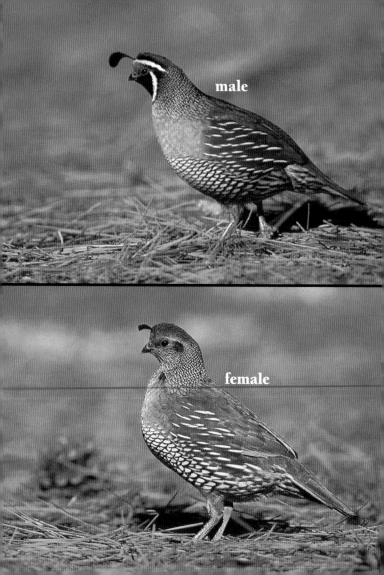

male

female

CALIFORNIA QUAIL
Callipepla californica

YEAR-ROUND

Size: 10" (25 cm)

Male: Plump gray quail with black face and chin. Prominent teardrop-shaped plume on the forehead. "Scaled" appearance on the belly, light brown to white. Pale brown forehead.

Female: similar to male, lacks a black face and chin

Juvenile: similar to female

Nest: ground; female builds; 1 brood per year

Eggs: 12-16; white with brown markings

Incubation: 18-23 days; female incubates

Fledging: 8-10 days; female and male teach young to feed

Migration: non-migrator

Food: seeds, leaves, insects; visits ground feeders

Compare: Male Gambel's Quail (pg. 293) is the same size with a rusty red crest and dark patch on the belly. Ring-necked Pheasant (pg. 233) is larger and lacks the plume on the head.

Stan's Notes: Prefers open fields, agricultural areas and sagebrush. Not found in dense forests or high elevations. Rarely flies, preferring to run away. Roosts in trees or dense shrubs at night, not on the ground. Usually seen in groups (coveys) of up to 100 individuals during winter, breaking up into small family units for breeding. Young stay with the family group until autumn. Has expanded its range in California over the past 50 years.

male

female

GAMBEL'S QUAIL
Callipepla gambelii

YEAR-ROUND

Size: 10" (25 cm)

Male: A plump round bird with a short tail. Gray chest, back and tail. Rusty crest outlined in white. Dark chin, throat and forehead with a unique dark plume emanating from the forehead. Rusty sides with white streaks. A dark patch on belly. Black bill. Gray legs.

Female: similar to male, lacks a rusty crest and dark chin, throat and forehead, plume less robust

Juvenile: similar to female

Nest: ground; female builds; 1-2 broods per year

Eggs: 8-12; dull white with brown markings

Incubation: 21-24 days; female incubates

Fledging: 7-10 days; female and male show the young what to eat

Migration: non-migrator

Food: seeds, leaves, insects, fruit; comes to seed feeders on the ground

Compare: California Quail (pg. 291) lacks the male's dark belly patch and rusty red crest.

Stan's Notes: A native species. Prefers arid scrubby regions with a constant water source. Winter flocks of up to 20 birds (coveys) split up during breeding season. Covey walks in single file. Able to hop on and over fences. Scurries across open areas to reach cover. Visits feeders in early morning and late afternoon. Takes dust baths in dirt depressions, kicking dust over body to get rid of small insects. Builds cup nest under vegetation, lining it with grass and feathers. Male gives a distinctive, repetitious call, "yup-waay-yup-yup."

breeding
pg. 51

winter

BLACK-BELLIED PLOVER
Pluvialis squatarola

WINTER

Size: 11-12" (28-30 cm)

Male: Winter plumage is uniform light gray with dark, nearly black streaks. White belly and chest. Faint white eyebrow mark. Black legs and bill.

Female: less black on belly and chest than male

Juvenile: grayer than adults, with much less black

Nest: ground; male and female construct; 1 brood per year

Eggs: 3-4; pinkish or greenish with black-brown markings

Incubation: 26-27 days; male and female incubate, the male during day, female at night

Fledging: 35-45 days; male feeds young, young learn quickly to feed themselves

Migration: complete, to coastal California, Mexico and Central and South America

Food: insects

Compare: Similar color as the winter Snowy Plover (pg. 361) and winter Sanderling (pg. 275), but much larger with a larger bill.

Stan's Notes: Males perform a "butterfly" courtship flight to attract females. Female leaves male and young about 12 days after the eggs hatch. Breeds at age 3. A common winter resident, arrivals begin in July and August (fall migration). Leaves in April. Doesn't breed in California. During flight, in any plumage, displays a white rump and stripe on the wings with black axillaries (armpits). Often darts across the ground to grab an insect and run.

CLARK'S NUTCRACKER
Nucifraga columbiana

YEAR-ROUND

Size: 12" (30 cm)

Male: Gray with black wings and a narrow black band down the center of tail. Small white patches on long wings, seen in flight. Has a relatively short tail with a white undertail.

Female: same as male

Juvenile: same as adult

Nest: cup; female and male build; 1 brood a year

Eggs: 2-5; pale green with brown markings

Incubation: 16-18 days; female and male incubate

Fledging: 18-20 days; female and male feed young

Migration: non-migrator

Food: seeds, insects, berries, eggs, mammals

Compare: Townsend's Solitaire (pg. 279) is smaller, lacks black wings and has a smaller bill. The Steller's Jay (pg. 93) is dark blue with a black crest. Female Phainopepla (pg. 277) has a crest and lacks a white undertail.

Stan's Notes: A high country bird found in coniferous forests in parts of California. It has a varied diet, but relies heavily on piñon seeds, frequently caching large amounts to consume later or feed to young. Has a large pouch in its throat (sublingual pouch), which it uses to transport seeds. Studies show the birds can carry up to 100 seeds at a time. Nests early in the year, often while snow still covers the ground, relying on stored foods. A "Lewis and Clark" bird, first recorded by William Clark in 1805 in Idaho.

soaring

juvenile

SHARP-SHINNED HAWK
Accipiter striatus

Size: 10-14" (25-36 cm); up to 2-foot wingspan

Male: Small woodland hawk with a gray back and head and a rusty red breast. Long tail with several dark tail bands, widest band at end of squared-off tail. Red eyes.

Female: same as male, only larger

Juvenile: same size as adults, with a brown back and heavily streaked breast, yellow eyes

Nest: platform; female builds; 1 brood per year

Eggs: 4-5; white with brown markings

Incubation: 32-35 days; female incubates

Fledging: 24-27 days; female and male feed young

Migration: complete to non-migrator in California

Food: birds, small mammals

Compare: Cooper's Hawk (pg. 307) is nearly identical, but larger and has a rounded tail. The Red-shouldered Hawk (pg. 195) has a reddish head and belly.

Stan's Notes: A common hawk of backyards and woodlands, often seen swooping in on birds visiting feeders. Its short rounded wings and long tail allow this hawk to navigate through thick stands of trees in pursuit of prey. Common name comes from the sharp keel on the leading edge of its "shin," though it is actually below rather than above the bird's ankle on the tarsus bone of foot. The tarsus in most birds is round. In flight, head doesn't protrude as far as the head of the Cooper's Hawk.

ROCK PIGEON
Columba livia

YEAR-ROUND

Size: 13" (33 cm)

Male: No set color pattern. Gray to white, patches of iridescent greens and blues, usually with a light rump patch.

Female: same as male

Juvenile: same as adult

Nest: platform; female builds; 3-4 broods a year

Eggs: 1-2; white without markings

Incubation: 18-20 days; female and male incubate

Fledging: 25-26 days; female and male feed young

Migration: non-migrator

Food: seeds

Compare: The larger Band-tailed Pigeon (pg. 303) is uniformly colored and patterned and has a disproportionately long tail. The Mourning Dove (pg. 171) is smaller, light brown and lacks all the color variations of Rock Pigeon.

Stan's Notes: Also known as Domestic Pigeon, it was introduced to North America from Europe by the early settlers. Most common around cities and barnyards, where it scratches for seeds. One of the few birds that has a wide variety of colors, produced by years of selective breeding while in captivity. Parents feed young a regurgitated liquid known as crop-milk the first few days of life. One of the few birds that can drink without tilting its head back. Nests under bridges and on buildings, balconies, barns and sheds. Was once poisoned as a "nuisance city bird." Many cities now have Peregrine Falcons (not shown) that feed on Rock Pigeons, keeping their numbers in check.

BAND-TAILED PIGEON
Patagioenas fasciata

YEAR-ROUND

Size: 14½" (37 cm)

Male: A typical pigeon-shaped body. Overall gray with a narrow white band on nape of neck. Dark eyes. Black-tipped yellow bill. Yellow legs. Disproportionately long tail.

Female: same as male

Juvenile: similar to adult, lacks white band on neck

Nest: cup; female and male construct; 2-3 broods per year

Eggs: 1-2; white without markings

Incubation: 18-20 days; female and male incubate

Fledging: 25-27 days; female and male feed young

Migration: non-migrator

Food: nuts, seeds, fruit, berries

Compare: The smaller Rock Pigeon (pg. 301) comes in a wide variety of colors and patterns unlike the uniformly colored and patterned Band-tailed. Look for a long tail, and the uniform color of Band-taileds in a flock.

Stan's Notes: A common pigeon in mountainous parts of the state. Has a nomadic lifestyle. Moves around constantly in response to the food supply. Often seen flying in groups. Male performs a courtship flight of rapid flapping alternating with short glides, then landing and bowing to female. Nests in scattered pairs. Easily distinguished from the Rock Pigeon by its uniform gray color and long tail.

**breeding
pg. 183**

displaying

winter

WILLET
Catoptrophorus semipalmatus

SUMMER
WINTER

Size: 15" (38 cm)

Male: Winter plumage is gray with a gray bill and legs. White belly. A distinctive black and white wing lining pattern, seen in flight or during display.

Female: same as male

Juvenile: similar to breeding adult, more tan in color

Nest: ground; female builds; 1 brood per year

Eggs: 3-5; olive green with dark markings

Incubation: 24-28 days; male and female incubate

Fledging: unknown days; female and male feed young

Migration: complete, to parts of California, the coast of Mexico, Central and South America

Food: aquatic insects

Compare: Slightly larger than the Greater Yellowlegs (pg. 179), which has yellow legs.

Stan's Notes: A common winter resident in California. Northern birds pass through coastal California to destinations farther south. Appearing a rich, warm brown during breeding season and rather plain gray in winter, it always has a striking black and white wing pattern when seen in flight. Uses its black and white wing patches to display to its mate. Named after the "pill-will-willet" call it gives during the breeding season. Gives a "kip-kip-kip" alarm call when it takes flight. It nests in far northeastern California, other western states, along the East coast and in Canada.

soaring

juvenile

COOPER'S HAWK
Accipiter cooperii

Size: 14-20" (36-50 cm); up to 2½-foot wingspan

Male: Medium-sized hawk with short wings and long rounded tail with several black bands. Rusty breast and dark wing tips. Slate gray back. Bright yellow spot at base of gray bill (cere). Dark red eyes.

Female: similar to male, only slightly larger

Juvenile: brown back with brown streaks on breast, bright yellow eyes

Nest: platform; male and female build; 1 brood per year

Eggs: 2-4; greenish with brown markings

Incubation: 32-36 days; female and male incubate

Fledging: 28-32 days; male and female feed young

Migration: non-migrator to partial migrator; will move around to find food

Food: small birds, mammals

Compare: Nearly identical to the Sharp-shinned Hawk (pg. 299), only larger, darker gray and with a rounded-off tail. Slimmer body and longer tail than Red-shouldered Hawk (pg. 195).

Stan's Notes: Common woodland hawk. In flight, look for its large head, short wings and long tail. The stubby wings help it maneuver between trees while pursuing small birds. This hawk will come to feeders, hunting for unaware birds. Flies with long glides followed by a few quick flaps. Known to ambush prey, it will fly into heavy brush or even run on the ground in pursuit. Nestlings have gray eyes that become bright yellow at 1 year of age and dark red later.

breeding

winter

juvenile

in flight
breeding

in flight
juvenile

HEERMANN'S GULL
Larus heermanni

MIGRATION WINTER

Size: 19" (48 cm); up to 4½-foot wingspan

Male: An overall dark gray gull with a white head. Distinctive darker wings and tail, both with white edges, as seen in flight. Black-tipped orange bill. Winter lacks a white head.

Female: same as male

Juvenile: light brown with a dark head and a black-tipped yellow bill

Nest: ground; female and male construct; 1 brood per year

Eggs: 2-3; dull white with brown markings

Incubation: 24-28 days; female and male incubate

Fledging: 28-30 days; female and male feed young

Migration: complete, to coastal California and Mexico, Central America

Food: fish, aquatic insects

Compare: California Gull (pg. 367) and Western Gull (pg. 369) are both larger and mostly white. Heermann's is the darkest gull on the beach.

Stan's Notes: One of the easiest gulls to identify due to its dark color. An unusual migratory dispersal with many moving up from Mexico, where they nest, to winter on the California coast. Nest is a shallow depression or scrape. Some are sparsely lined. Some nest in tall grass, smashing down plants to create a cup. Nest is usually on isolated islands or coastal flats. Juveniles are light brown through the first winter. Second-year birds are dark gray to brown. Achieves breeding plumage in third year. Fewer than 1 in 250 breeding birds have a conspicuous white patch on their wings, as seen in flight.

male

female pg. 219

NORTHERN HARRIER
Circus cyaneus

YEAR-ROUND
WINTER

Size: 20" (50 cm); up to 3½-foot wingspan

Male: A slim, low-flying hawk. Silver gray with a large white rump patch and a white belly. Faint narrow bands across the tail. Tips of wings black. Yellow eyes.

Female: dark brown back, a brown-streaked breast and belly, large white rump patch, narrow black bands across tail, tips of wings black, yellow eyes

Juvenile: similar to female, with an orange breast

Nest: platform, often on ground; female and male build; 1 brood per year

Eggs: 4-8; bluish white without markings

Incubation: 31-32 days; female incubates

Fledging: 30-35 days; male and female feed young

Migration: non-migrator to partial in California

Food: mice, snakes, insects, small birds

Compare: Slimmer than Red-tailed Hawk (pg. 221). Look for black bands on tail and a white rump patch.

Stan's Notes: One of the easiest hawks to identify. Harriers glide just above ground, following contours of the land while searching for prey. Holds its wings just above the horizontal position, tilting back and forth in the wind, similar to Turkey Vultures. Formerly called Marsh Hawk due to its habit of hunting over marshes. Feeds on the ground. Will perch on the ground to preen and rest. At any age, has a distinctive owl-like face disk.

female pg. 213

male

GADWALL
Anas strepera

YEAR-ROUND
WINTER

Size: 20" (50 cm)

Male: A plump gray duck with a brown head and a distinctive black rump. White belly and chestnut-tinged wings. Bright white wing linings. Small white wing patch, seen when swimming. Gray bill.

Female: similar to female Mallard, a mottled brown with a pronounced color change from dark brown body to light brown neck and head, bright white wing linings, small white wing patch, gray bill with orange sides

Juvenile: similar to female

Nest: ground; female lines the nest with fine grass and down feathers plucked from her chest; 1 brood per year

Eggs: 8-11; white without markings

Incubation: 24-27 days; female incubates

Fledging: 48-56 days; young feed themselves

Migration: complete to non-migrator in California

Food: aquatic insects

Compare: Male Gadwall is one of the few gray ducks. Look for its distinctive black rump.

Stan's Notes: A duck of shallow marshes. Consumes mostly plant material, dunking its head in water to feed rather than tipping forward, like other dabbling ducks. Walks well on land; feeds in fields and woodlands. Frequently in pairs with other duck species. Nests within 300 feet (100 m) of water. Establishes pair bond in winter.

in flight

CANADA GOOSE
Branta canadensis

**YEAR-ROUND
WINTER**

Size: 25-43" (63-109 cm); up to 5½-foot wingspan

Male: Large gray goose with black neck and head, with a white chin or cheek strap.

Female: same as male

Juvenile: same as adult

Nest: platform, on the ground; female builds; 1 brood per year

Eggs: 5-10; white without markings

Incubation: 25-30 days; female incubates

Fledging: 42-55 days; male and female teach young to feed

Migration: partial to complete, to California; will move to any place with open water

Food: aquatic plants, insects, seeds

Compare: Large goose that is rarely confused with any other bird.

Stan's Notes: Winter resident in California. Adults mate for many years, but only start to breed in their third year. Males frequently act as sentinels, standing at the edge of the group, bobbing their heads up and down, becoming very aggressive to anybody who approaches. Will hiss as if displaying displeasure. Adults molt their primary flight feathers while raising young, rendering family groups flightless at the same time. Several subspecies vary geographically across the U.S. Generally they are darker in color in western groups and paler in eastern. Size decreases northward, with the smallest subspecies found on the Arctic tundra.

in flight

SANDHILL CRANE
Grus canadensis

Size: 40-48" (102-120 cm); up to 7-foot wingspan

Male: Elegant gray bird with long legs and neck. Wings and body often stained rusty brown. Scarlet red cap. Yellow-to-red eyes.

Female: same as male

Juvenile: dull brown, lacks red cap, has yellow eyes

Nest: platform, on the ground; female and male build; 1 brood per year

Eggs: 2; olive with brown markings

Incubation: 28-32 days; female and male incubate

Fledging: 65 days; female and male feed young

Migration: complete, to parts of California, Mexico

Food: insects, fruit, worms, plants, amphibians

Compare: Similar size as Great Blue Heron (pg. 319), but the Crane has a shorter bill and red cap. Great Blue Heron flies with neck held in an S shape unlike the Crane's straight neck.

Stan's Notes: Among the tallest birds in the world and capable of flying at great heights. Usually seen in large undisturbed fields near water. Often heard before seen, they have a very distinctive rattling call. Plumage often appears rust brown because of staining from mud during preening. Characteristic flight with upstroke quicker than down. For their spectacular mating dance the performers face each other, bow and jump into the air while uttering loud cackling sounds and flapping wings. Often flips sticks and grass into the air during dance. Summers in northeastern California, spending the winter in other parts of the state.

in flight

GREAT BLUE HERON
Ardea herodias

YEAR-ROUND

Size: 42-52" (107-132 cm); up to 6-foot wingspan

Male: Tall gray heron. Black eyebrows extend into several long plumes off the back of head. Long yellow bill. Feathers at base of neck drop down in a kind of necklace.

Female: same as male

Juvenile: same as adult, but more brown than gray, with a black crown and no plumes

Nest: platform; male and female build; 1 brood per year

Eggs: 3-5; blue green without markings

Incubation: 27-28 days; female and male incubate

Fledging: 56-60 days; male and female feed young

Migration: non-migrator in California

Food: small fish, frogs, insects, snakes

Compare: Similar size as the Sandhill Crane (pg. 317), but lacks the Crane's red crown. Crane flies with neck held straight unlike the Heron's S-shaped neck.

Stan's Notes: One of the most common herons, often barking like a dog when startled. Seen stalking small fish in shallow water. Will strike at mice, squirrels and just about anything else it might come across. Flies holding neck in an S shape, with its long legs trailing straight out behind. The wings are held in cupped fashion during flight. Nests in colonies of up to 100 birds. Nests in treetops near or over open water. A year-round resident. Populations increase when birds north of California migrate to spend the winter.

male

female

CALLIOPE HUMMINGBIRD
Stellula calliope

Size: 3¼" (8 cm)

Male: Iridescent green head, back and tail. Breast and belly white to tan. Iridescent rosy red throat patch (gorget), V-shaped. Compared with other hummingbirds, has a very short, thin bill and a short tail. Wing tips reach to tip of tail.

Female: same as male, but thin, spotty throat patch

Juvenile: similar to female

Nest: cup; female builds; 1 brood per year

Eggs: 1-2; white without markings

Incubation: 15-17 days; female incubates

Fledging: 18-22 days; female feeds young

Migration: complete, to Central and South America

Food: nectar, insects; will come to nectar feeders

Compare: Smaller than the other hummingbirds. Look for the short thin bill and short tail, with the tips of wings extending past the tail. Female is similar to the female Anna's (pg. 327) and Rufous (pg. 345), but Calliope has a shorter, thinner bill and short tail.

Stan's Notes: Smallest bird in North America. Common in open forests and brushy areas in lower elevations of the state. A relatively quiet bird, it will come to nectar feeders. During breeding season, males can be heard zinging around while displaying for females. Females are hard to distinguish from other female hummingbirds. Often builds nest on branches of pine trees. Juvenile males obtain a partial throat patch by autumn of their first year.

male

female

COSTA'S HUMMINGBIRD
Calypte costae

YEAR-ROUND
SUMMER

Size: 3½" (9 cm)

Male: Green back and nape, white belly and light green flanks. Dark crown, chin, throat and down the neck, like a handlebar mustache. In direct sunlight, dark area around head reflects iridescent purple. White eyebrows.

Female: same as male, without dark marks on head, has white marks around eyes, gray cheeks

Juvenile: similar to female

Nest: cup; female builds; 1 brood per year

Eggs: 2; white without markings

Incubation: 15-18 days; female incubates

Fledging: 20-23 days; female feeds young

Migration: partial migrator to non-migrator, to Mexico

Food: small insects, flower nectar; visits feeders

Compare: Smaller size and shorter tail than most other hummers in California. Look for the male's purple cap and mustache marks on throat. Identify the female Costa's by its gray cheeks and white markings around each eye. Wings extend just beyond tip of tail when perched.

Stan's Notes: Good lighting is needed to see the green iridescence. Some stay the winter if a consistent food source is available such as a hummingbird feeder. Actively defends itself and is very territorial. Often perches, guarding territory and food supply. Gives a limited song, "tink-tink-tink," as it chases other hummers. Male performs an elaborate diving flight display to attract a mate. After mating, the female moves to her own territory to build nest and raise young.

male

female

BLACK-CHINNED HUMMINGBIRD
Archilochus alexandri

MIGRATION
SUMMER

Size: 3¾" (9.5 cm)

Male: Tiny iridescent green bird with black throat patch (gorget) that reflects violet blue in sunlight. Black chin. White chest and belly.

Female: same as male, but lacking the throat patch and black chin, has white flanks

Juvenile: similar to female

Nest: cup; female builds; 1-2 broods per year

Eggs: 1-3; white without markings

Incubation: 13-16 days; female incubates

Fledging: 19-21 days; female feeds young

Migration: complete, to Central and South America

Food: nectar, insects; will come to nectar feeders

Compare: Larger than Costa's (pg. 323), but lacking the handlebar mustache gorget. The male Black-chinned Hummingbird often appears to have an all-black head.

Stan's Notes: One of several hummingbird species in California. Able to fly backward, but doesn't sing. Will chatter or buzz to communicate. Wings create a humming noise, flapping nearly 80 times per second. Weighing 2-3 grams, it takes about five average-sized hummingbirds to equal the weight of one chickadee. Males return first at the end of April. Male performs a spectacular pendulum-like flight over a perched female. After mating, the female builds a nest, using spider webs to glue nest materials together, and raises young without mate's help. More than one clutch per year not uncommon.

male

female

ANNA'S HUMMINGBIRD
Calypte anna

Size: 4" (10 cm)

Male: Iridescent green body with dark head, chin and neck. In direct sunlight, the dark head shines a deep rose red. Breast and belly are dull gray. White eye-ring.

Female: similar to male, but head reflects only a few red flecks instead of a complete rose red

Juvenile: similar to female

Nest: cup; female builds; 2-3 broods per year

Eggs: 1-3; white without markings

Incubation: 14-19 days; female incubates

Fledging: 18-23 days; female feeds young

Migration: partial to non-migrator; many move to the coast of southern California and Mexico

Food: nectar, insects; will come to nectar feeders

Compare: Anna's is similar to other hummers, but the male has a completely dark head and white eye-ring. Female has a few red flecks on the throat. Tail extends well beyond wing tips when perched.

Stan's Notes: Common western hummingbird found from Baja, California, to British Columbia. Unknown in California before the late 1950s, it has since expanded northward and is now considered common. An early nester. Female builds a tiny nest on chaparral-covered hillsides and in canyons. Feathers on head are black until seen in direct sun. Reflected sunlight turns the male's head bright rosy red. Apparently consumes more insects than other species of hummingbirds. Generally non-migratory; some may migrate.

YEAR-ROUND
SUMMER

GREEN-TAILED TOWHEE
Pipilo chlorurus

MIGRATION
SUMMER

Size: 7¼" (18.5 cm)

Male: A unique yellowish green back, wings and tail. Dark gray chest and face. Bright white throat with black stripes. Rusty red crown.

Female: same as male

Juvenile: olive green with heavy streaking on breast and belly, lacks crown and throat markings of adult

Nest: cup; female and male construct; 1-2 broods per year

Eggs: 3-5; white with brown markings

Incubation: 12-14 days; female and male incubate

Fledging: 10-14 days; female and male feed young

Migration: complete, to Mexico and Central America

Food: insects, seeds, fruit

Compare: California Towhee (pg. 155) is larger and lacks the rusty red crown and bright white chin and throat. The Green-tailed's unusual color, short wings, long tail and large bill make it easy to identify.

Stan's Notes: Common summer resident of shrubby hillsides and sagebrush mountain slopes up to 7,000 feet (2,150 m). Like other towhee species, searches for insects and seeds, taking a little jump forward while kicking backward with both feet. Known to scurry away from trouble, jumping to ground without opening its wings and running across the ground.

LEWIS'S WOODPECKER
Melanerpes lewis

Size: 10¾" (27.5 cm)

Male: Dull green head and back. Distinctive gray collar and breast. Deep red face and a light red belly.

Female: same as male

Juvenile: similar to adult, with a brown head, lacking the red face

Nest: cavity; male and female excavate; 1 brood per year

Eggs: 4-8; white without markings

Incubation: 13-14 days; female and male incubate

Fledging: 28-34 days; female and male feed young

Migration: partial migrator to non-migrator; will move around to find food in winter

Food: insects, nuts, seeds, berries

Compare: Acorn Woodpecker (pg. 45) has white on the head and a red cap. Male Williamson's Sapsucker (pg. 47) has a black back and large white wing patches.

Stan's Notes: Large and handsome woodpecker of western states. First collected and named in 1805 by Lewis and Clark in Montana. During breeding season, it feeds exclusively on insects rather than grubs, like other woodpeckers. Prefers open pine forests and areas with recent forest fires. Excavates in dead or soft wood. Uses same cavity year after year. Tends to mate for long term. Moves around in winter to search for food such as pine nuts (seeds).

female pg. 205

male

WOOD DUCK
Aix sponsa

YEAR-ROUND
SUMMER
WINTER

Size: 17-20" (43-50 cm)

Male: A small, highly ornamented dabbling duck with a green head and crest patterned with white and black. A rusty chest, white belly and red eyes.

Female: brown, similar size and shape as male, has bright white eye-ring and a not-so-obvious crest, blue patch on wing often hidden

Juvenile: same as female

Nest: cavity; female lines old woodpecker cavity; 1 brood per year

Eggs: 10-15; creamy white without markings

Incubation: 28-36 days; female incubates

Fledging: 56-68 days; female teaches young to feed

Migration: non-migrator to partial in California

Food: aquatic insects, plants, seeds

Compare: More colorful than male Green-winged Teal (pg. 187). Smaller than the male Shoveler (pg. 339) and lacks the long wide bill.

Stan's Notes: A common duck of quiet, shallow backwater ponds. Nearly extinct around 1900 due to overhunting, but is doing well now. Nests in an old woodpecker hole or uses a nesting box. Often seen flying deep in forests or perched high on tree branches. Female takes to flight with a loud squealing call and enters nest cavity from full flight. Lays eggs in a neighboring female nest (egg dumping), resulting in some clutches in excess of 20 eggs. Young stay in nest 24 hours after hatching, then jump from up to 30 feet (9 m) to the ground or water to follow their mother, never returning to the nest.

GREEN HERON
Butorides virescens

YEAR-ROUND
MIGRATION
SUMMER

Size: 16-22" (40-56 cm)

Male: Short stocky heron with a blue-green back, and rusty red neck and chest. Dark green crest. Short legs, normally yellow, but turn bright orange during breeding season.

Female: same as male

Juvenile: similar to adult, with a blue-gray back and white-streaked chest and neck

Nest: platform; female and male build; 2 broods per year

Eggs: 2-4; light green without markings

Incubation: 21-25 days; female and male incubate

Fledging: 35-36 days; female and male feed young

Migration: complete to non-migrator in California

Food: fish, insects, aquatic plants

Compare: Much smaller than the Great Blue Heron (pg. 319) and lacks the long neck of most other herons. Look for a small heron with a dark green back stalking wetlands.

Stan's Notes: Often gives an explosive, rasping "skyew" call when startled. Sometimes it looks like it doesn't have a neck, because it holds its head close to its body. Hunts for fish and aquatic insects by waiting along a shore or wades stealthily. Has been known to place an object, such as an insect, on the water surface to attract fish to catch. Raises its crest when excited.

female pg. 211

male

MALLARD
Anas platyrhynchos

YEAR-ROUND

Size: 19-21" (48-53 cm)

Male: Large, bulbous green head, white necklace and rust brown or chestnut chest. Gray and white on the sides. Yellow bill. Orange legs and feet.

Female: all brown with orange and black bill, small blue and white wing mark (speculum)

Juvenile: same as female, but with a yellow bill

Nest: ground; female builds; 1 brood per year

Eggs: 7-10; greenish to whitish, unmarked

Incubation: 26-30 days; female incubates

Fledging: 42-52 days; female leads young to food

Migration: non-migrator to partial in California

Food: seeds, plants, aquatic insects; will come to ground feeders offering corn

Compare: The male Northern Shoveler (pg. 339) has a white chest with rust on sides and a dark spoon-shaped bill. Breeding male Northern Pintail (pg. 215) has long tail feathers and a brown head. Male Red-breasted Merganser (pg. 341) has a shaggy crest and orange bill.

Stan's Notes: A familiar duck of lakes and ponds, it's considered a type of dabbling duck, tipping forward in shallow water to feed on aquatic plants on the bottom. The name "Mallard" comes from the Latin *masculus*, meaning "male," referring to the habit of males not taking part in raising ducklings. Black central tail feathers of male curl upward. Both the male and female have white tails and white underwings. Will return to place of birth.

female pg. 217

male

NORTHERN SHOVELER
Anas clypeata

MIGRATION
WINTER

Size: 20" (50 cm)

Male: Medium-sized duck with iridescent green head, rusty sides and white breast. Has an extraordinarily large spoon-shaped bill that is almost always held pointed toward water.

Female: same spoon-shaped bill, brown and black all over and green speculum

Juvenile: same as female

Nest: ground; female builds; 1 brood per year

Eggs: 9-12; olive without markings

Incubation: 22-25 days; female incubates

Fledging: 30-60 days; female leads young to food

Migration: complete, to California, Mexico and Central America

Food: aquatic insects, plants

Compare: Similar to the male Mallard (pg. 337), but Shoveler has a large, characteristic spoon-shaped bill. Larger than male Wood Duck (pg. 333) and lacks the Wood Duck's crest.

Stan's Notes: One of several species of shoveler, so called because of the peculiar shape of its bill. The Northern Shoveler is the only species of these ducks in North America. Found in small flocks of 5-10, swimming low in water with its large bill pointed toward the water, as if it's too heavy to lift. Feeds mainly by filtering tiny aquatic insects and plants from the water's surface with its bill. Winters in California where it can find water.

female pg. 229

male

RED-BREASTED MERGANSER
Mergus serrator

MIGRATION
WINTER

Size: 23" (58 cm)

Male: A shaggy green head and crest. Prominent white collar. Rusty breast. Black and white body. Long orange bill.

Female: overall brown to gray with a shaggy reddish head and crest, long orange bill

Juvenile: similar to female

Nest: ground; female builds; 1 brood per year

Eggs: 5-10; olive green without markings

Incubation: 29-30 days; female incubates

Fledging: 55-65 days; female feeds young

Migration: complete, to coastal California, Mexico and Central America

Food: fish, aquatic insects

Compare: Larger than the male Hooded Merganser (pg. 63), which has a large white patch on the head unlike the green head of the male Red-breasted Merganser.

Stan's Notes: A very fast flier, clocked at up to 100 miles (161 km) per hour. Often seen flying low across the water. Needs a long take-off run with wings flapping to get airborne. Serrated bill helps it catch slippery fish. Usually a silent duck. Male sometimes gives a soft, catlike meow. Female gives a harsh "krrr-croak." Doesn't breed before 2 years of age. Male abandons female just after eggs are laid. Females often share a nest. Breeds in Alaska and northern Canada. Young leave the nest within 24 hours of hatching, never to return.

male

female

MIGRATION
SUMMER

ALLEN'S HUMMINGBIRD
Selasphorus sasin

Size: 3¾" (9.5 cm)

Male: Rusty orange cheeks, chest, belly, rump and tail. Iridescent green cap, back and upper surface of wings. Long, thin dark bill. Small white patch in center of breast, just under throat patch (gorget). A nearly black gorget, turning reddish orange in direct sunlight.

Female: similar to male, but much less orange, solid green back and tail, small reddish orange flecks on throat, lacks the large throat patch

Juvenile: similar to female, with a white chin

Nest: cup; female builds; 1-2 broods per year

Eggs: 2; white without markings

Incubation: 17-22 days; female incubates

Fledging: 22-25 days; female feeds young

Migration: complete, to Mexico and Central America

Food: nectar, insects; will come to nectar feeders

Compare: Male Rufous (pg. 345) has an orange back and crown. Rufous and Allen's females are nearly identical, but Rufous is usually seen during migration and winter.

Stan's Notes: Male performs for perching female, swooping up to 75 feet (23 m) in a J shape, giving a buzzing call at the bottom. After mating, female builds a small nest of plant fibers on the top of a tree limb. She camouflages the outside with lichen bits and binds it with spider silk, often completing it in 10-12 days. Hummingbirds often lay only two eggs. Female defends nest area from most birds. Adult males migrate first in fall. Females and young follow a month later.

male

female

RUFOUS HUMMINGBIRD
Selasphorus rufus

MIGRATION
WINTER

Size: 3¾" (9.5 cm)

Male: Tiny burnt orange bird with a black throat patch (gorget) that reflects orange-red in sunlight. White chest. Green-to-tan flanks.

Female: same as male, but lacking the throat patch

Juvenile: similar to female

Nest: cup; female builds; 1-2 broods per year

Eggs: 1-3; white without markings

Incubation: 14-17 days; female incubates

Fledging: 21-26 days; female feeds young

Migration: complete, to Central and South America

Food: nectar, insects; will come to nectar feeders

Compare: Identified by its unique orange-red (rufous) color. Very similar to Allen's Hummingbird (pg. 343), but male Allen's has a green back and cap. Females are nearly identical, but the Allen's is seen in summer.

Stan's Notes: This is a bold, hardy hummer. Often seen well out of its normal range in the western U.S., showing up along the East coast. Visits hummingbird feeders in your yard during migration. Doesn't sing, but will chatter or buzz to communicate. Weighing just 2-3 grams, it takes about five average-sized hummingbirds to equal the weight of a single chickadee. Heart pumps an incredible 1,260 beats per minute. Male performs a spectacular pendulum-like flight over the perched female. After mating, the female flies off to build a nest and raise young, without any help from her mate. Constructs a soft, flexible nest that expands to accommodate the growing young. Doesn't nest in California.

female pg. 397

male

BULLOCK'S ORIOLE
Icterus bullockii

SUMMER

Size: 8" (20 cm)

Male: Bright orange and black bird. Black crown, eye line, nape, chin, back and wings with a bold white patch on wings.

Female: dull yellow overall, pale white belly, white wing bars on gray-to-black wings

Juvenile: similar to female

Nest: pendulous; female and male build; 1 brood per year

Eggs: 4-6; pale white to gray, brown markings

Incubation: 12-14 days; female incubates

Fledging: 12-14 days; female and male feed young

Migration: complete, to Central and South America

Food: insects, berries, nectar; visits nectar feeders

Compare: A handsome bird. Look for male Bullock's bright orange and black markings, and thin black line running through the eyes. Male Hooded Oriole (pg. 349) is the same size, but lacks the black crown and nape.

Stan's Notes: So closely related to Baltimore Orioles of the eastern U.S., at one time both were considered a single species. Interbreeds with Baltimores where their ranges overlap. Most common in the state where cottonwood trees grow along rivers and other wetlands. Also found at edges of clearings, in city parks, on farms and along irrigation ditches. Hanging sock-like nest is constructed of plant fibers such as inner bark of junipers and willows. Will incorporate yarn and thread into its nest if offered at the time of nest building.

female pg. 399

male

SUMMER

HOODED ORIOLE
Icterus cucullatus

Size: 8" (20 cm)

Male: Orange yellow head, nape, chest, rump and belly. Black face, chin, throat, bill and eyes. Large white wing bar. Dark wings and tail.

Female: dull yellow with gray wings and back

Juvenile: similar to adult of the same sex

Nest: pendulous; female and male construct; 1-2 broods per year

Eggs: 3-5; dull white with brown markings

Incubation: 12-14 days; female incubates

Fledging: 12-14 days; female and male feed young

Migration: complete, to Central and South America

Food: insects, fruit, nectar

Compare: Male Bullock's Oriole (pg. 347) is the same size, but has a black crown and nape. Male Scott's Oriole (pg. 401) is larger and has a black head and chest.

Stan's Notes: A bird of tree-lined creeks and streams, palm groves, mesquite and arid scrub, often near suburbs. Male courts female with bows while hopping around her, singing a soft song. Points his bill skyward (like many birds in the blackbird family). Female will respond with a similar dance. Constructs an unusual sock-like nest, hung from a twig or woven through a palm leaf. Entrance often near the top, but can be on the side. Takes 3-7 days to build nest of wiry green grass, shredded palm leaves or yucca fibers. Some repair and reuse nests. Sips flower nectar, but not like hummingbirds. Often slices into the base of a flower, bypassing its natural entrance. Young are fed a regurgitate of insects and nectar the first 5-7 days of life.

female pg. 145

male

BLACK-HEADED GROSBEAK
Pheucticus melanocephalus

MIGRATION
SUMMER

Size: 8" (20 cm)

Male: Stocky bird with burnt orange chest, neck and rump. Black head, tail and wings with irregular-shaped white wing patches. Large bill with upper bill darker than lower.

Female: appears like an overgrown sparrow, overall brown with a lighter breast and belly, large two-toned bill, prominent white eyebrows, yellow wing linings, as seen in flight

Juvenile: similar to adult of the same sex

Nest: cup; female builds; 1 brood per year

Eggs: 3-4; pale green or bluish, brown markings

Incubation: 11-13 days; female and male incubate

Fledging: 11-13 days; female and male feed young

Migration: complete, to Mexico, Central America and South America

Food: seeds, insects, fruit; comes to seed feeders

Compare: Male Bullock's Oriole (pg. 347) has more white on wings than male Black-headed. Look for Black-headed's large bicolored bill.

Stan's Notes: A cosmopolitan bird that nests in a wide variety of habitats. Both males and females sing and aggressively defend their nests against intruders. Song is very similar to the American Robin's and Western Tanager's, making it hard to tell them apart by song. Populations are increasing in California and across the U.S.

male

female

VARIED THRUSH
Ixoreus naevius

Size: 9½" (24 cm)

Male: Potbellied robin-like bird with orange eyebrows, chin, breast and wing bars. Head, neck and back are gray to blue. Black breast band and eye mark.

Female: browner version of male, lacking the black breast band

Juvenile: similar to female

Nest: cup; female builds; 1-2 broods per year

Eggs: 3-5; pale blue with brown markings

Incubation: 12-14 days; female incubates

Fledging: 10-15 days; female and male feed young

Migration: complete, to California

Food: insects, fruit

Compare: Similar size and shape as American Robin (pg. 287), but Thrush has a warm orange breast unlike the red breast of Robin. Male Thrush has a distinctive black breast band.

Stan's Notes: An intriguing-looking bird. Nests in Alaska, Canada and the mountains of the U.S. Northwest. Prefers moist coniferous forests. It is most common in dense, older coniferous forests in high elevations. Moves to lower elevations in the winter where it is often seen in towns, orchards or thickets. Seen during winter in flocks of up to 20 birds. Well known for individual birds to fly eastward in winter, showing up in nearly any state, then returning to the Pacific Northwest for breeding.

yellow male

female pg. 105

male

HOUSE FINCH
Carpodacus mexicanus

YEAR-ROUND

Size: 5" (13 cm)

Male: An orange red face, breast and rump, with a brown cap. Brown marking behind eyes. Brown wings streaked with white. A white belly with brown streaks.

Female: brown with a heavily streaked white chest

Juvenile: similar to female

Nest: cup, sometimes in cavities; female builds; 2 broods per year

Eggs: 4-5; pale blue, lightly marked

Incubation: 12-14 days; female incubates

Fledging: 15-19 days; female and male feed young

Migration: non-migrator; moves around to find food

Food: seeds, fruit, leaf buds; will visit seed feeders

Compare: The male Vermilion Flycatcher (pg. 357) has a black nape, back and wings.

Stan's Notes: Very social bird. Visits feeders in small flocks. Likes nesting in hanging flower baskets. Incubating female fed by male. Loud, cheerful warbling song. Suffers a fatal eye disease that causes eyes to crust over. Historically it occurred from the Pacific coast to the Rocky Mountains, with a few reaching the eastern side. Birds introduced to Long Island, New York, in the 1940s have populated the entire eastern U.S. Now found throughout the U.S. Can be the most common bird at your feeders. Rarely, some males are yellow (see inset) instead of red, probably due to poor diet.

female pg. 265

male

VERMILION FLYCATCHER
Pyrocephalus rubinus

**YEAR-ROUND
SUMMER**

Size: 6" (15 cm)

Male: A stunningly beautiful bird with a crimson red head, crest, chin, breast and belly. Black nape, back, wings and tail. Thick black line running through eyes. Thin black bill.

Female: gray head, neck and back, nearly white chin and breast, pink belly to undertail, black tail, thin black bill

Juvenile: similar to female, lacks a pink undertail

Nest: cup; female builds; 1-2 broods per year

Eggs: 2-4; white with brown markings

Incubation: 14-16 days; female and male incubate

Fledging: 14-16 days; female and male feed young

Migration: complete migrator to non-migrator in parts of southern California

Food: insects (mainly bees)

Compare: The unique bright crimson plumage with black wings make this bird easy to identify.

Stan's Notes: A uniquely colored flycatcher that is often found in open areas with shrubs and small trees close to water. Feeds mainly on insects, with bees making up a large part of its diet. Will perch on a thin branch, pumping tail up and down while waiting for an aerial insect. Flies out to snatch it up, then returns to perch. Drops to the ground for terrestrial insects. Male raises its crest, fluffs chest feathers, fans tail and sings a song during a fluttery flight to court females. Female builds a shallow nest of twigs and grasses and lines it with downy plant material. Male feeds female during incubation and brooding.

female pg. 207

male

REDHEAD
Aythya americana

YEAR-ROUND
WINTER

Size: 19" (48 cm)

Male: Rich red head and neck with a black breast and tail. Gray sides. Smoky gray wings and back. Tricolored bill with a light blue base, white ring and black tip.

Female: plain, soft brown duck with gray-to-white wing linings, top of head rounded, gray bill with black tip

Juvenile: similar to female

Nest: cup; female builds; 1 brood per year

Eggs: 9-14; pale white without markings

Incubation: 24-28 days; female and male incubate

Fledging: 56-73 days; female shows the young what to eat

Migration: complete to non-migrator in California

Food: seeds, aquatic plants, insects

Compare: The male Northern Shoveler (pg. 339) has a green head and rusty sides unlike the male Redhead's gray sides.

Stan's Notes: A duck of permanent large bodies of water. Forages along the shoreline, feeding on seeds, aquatic plants and insects. Usually builds nest directly on surface of water, using large mats of vegetation. Female lays up to 75 percent of its eggs in the nests of other Redheads and several other duck species. Nests primarily in the Prairie Pothole region of the northern Great Plains. The overall populations seem to be increasing at about 2-3 percent each year. Winters throughout California where it can find water.

breeding

winter

SNOWY PLOVER
Charadrius alexandrinus

YEAR-ROUND
SUMMER

Size: 6¼" (15.5 cm)

Male: Small shorebird with pale white face, nape, chin, chest, belly and undertail. Black patch on forehead, each side of neck and behind each eye. Small dark bill. Gray legs and feet. Winter plumage lacks black markings.

Female: same as male

Juvenile: similar to winter adult

Nest: ground; male builds; 1-2 broods per year

Eggs: 2-3; buff white with brown markings

Incubation: 25-32 days; male and female incubate

Fledging: 30-32 days; male and female teach young what to eat

Migration: partial to non-migrator, from inland to the California coast and Mexico

Food: insects, worms, tiny fish

Compare: Killdeer (pg. 165) is larger with 2 distinct black bands around neck and upper chest. The breeding Black-bellied Plover (pg. 51) is larger with a black belly, chest and face.

Stan's Notes: The smallest, whitest North American plover. Often on beaches, mud and salt flats, fields and farms. In pairs during breeding season, groups at other times. Unique feeding behavior. Runs a few quick steps, then stops to look for moving prey. Vibrates legs and feet to scare up prey. Male displays to female at nest. Bows forward, points bill at nest, raises wings and ruffles feathers. Builds several nests, but uses one. Female leaves six days after eggs hatch. Male cares for young for a month. One in three females mates again.

361

winter

in flight

breeding

BONAPARTE'S GULL
Larus philadelphia

Size: 13½" (34.5 cm); up to 3-foot wingspan

Male: Mostly white during breeding season (April to August) with gray upper surface of wings and back. Black head, small black bill and white crescent marks around eyes. Black tips of wings and tail, seen in flight. Winter lacks a black head and has a dark ear spot.

Female: same as male

Juvenile: similar to winter male

Nest: platform; female and male construct; 1-2 broods per year

Eggs: 2-4; light brown with brown markings

Incubation: 20-24 days; female and male incubate

Fledging: 21-25 days; female and male feed young

Migration: complete, to coastal California and Mexico

Food: aquatic and terrestrial insects, fish

Compare: California Gull (pg. 367) and Western Gull (pg. 369) are larger and lack the breeding Bonaparte's black head. Look for the small black bill to help identify Bonaparte's Gull.

Stan's Notes: Rarely with other gull species, presumably due to its small size. California is home to some of the highest concentrations of this species in the U.S. Rarely found away from the coast during winter, but on lakes and rivers during migration. Said to resemble a tern species due to its small size, short thin bill and swift flight. It nests across Canada and southern Alaska where there is water. Builds its own nest or takes an abandoned nest in a tree, mainly conifers. Takes two years for young to obtain adult plumage.

363

winter

in flight

breeding

juvenile

RING-BILLED GULL
Larus delawarensis

Size: 19" (48 cm); up to 4-foot wingspan

Male: A white bird with gray wings, black wing tips spotted with white, and a white tail, as seen in flight. Yellow bill with a black ring near tip. Yellowish legs and feet. Winter or non-breeding adult has a speckled brown back of head and nape of neck.

Female: same as male

Juvenile: mostly gray version of winter adult, has a dark band at end of tail

Nest: ground; female and male construct; 1 brood per year

Eggs: 2-4; off-white with brown markings

Incubation: 20-21 days; female and male incubate

Fledging: 20-40 days; female and male feed young

Migration: complete, to California and Mexico

Food: insects, fish; scavenges for food

Compare: Smaller than the California Gull (pg. 367) and lacks breeding California's red mark on bill. Smaller than Western Gull (pg. 369), which has an orange dot on bill. Look for a black ring around the bill near the tip.

Stan's Notes: A common gull of garbage dumps and parking lots. It's expanding its range and remaining farther north longer during winter due to successful scavenging in cities. A three-year gull with a new, different plumage in each of the first three autumns. Attains ring on bill after its first winter and adult plumage in its third year. Defends a small area around nest.

juvenile

winter

in flight

breeding

CALIFORNIA GULL
Larus californicus

YEAR-ROUND
MIGRATION
SUMMER
WINTER

Size: 21" (53 cm); up to 4½-foot wingspan

Male: White bird with gray wings and black wing tips. A red and black mark on tip of yellow bill. Red ring around dark eyes. Winter or non-breeding adult has brown streaks on back of head and nape of neck.

Female: same as male

Juvenile: all brown for the first two years, similar to winter adult by the third year

Nest: ground; female and male construct; 1 brood per year

Eggs: 2-5; pale brown or olive, brown markings

Incubation: 24-26 days; female and male incubate

Fledging: 40-45 days; female and male feed young

Migration: complete, to parts of California, the coast of Mexico

Food: insects, seeds, mammals

Compare: The Western Gull (pg. 369) lacks the black mark on the mandible. Breeding Bonaparte's Gull (pg. 363) has a black head.

Stan's Notes: This is the famed gull species that saved crops from overpopulations of grasshoppers during 1848 and inspired the gull monuments in Salt Lake City. A four-year gull that appears nearly all brown during the first two years. Third-year bird is similar to the winter adult. Usually doesn't nest until the fourth year, when it obtains adult plumage. Nests in large colonies of up to 1,000 nests in Idaho, Montana, western Canada and other areas. Common on reservoirs. Named for its usual winter sites on the California coast.

winter

in flight
juvenile

breeding

in flight

WESTERN GULL
Larus occidentalis

YEAR-ROUND

Size: 24" (60 cm); up to 5-foot wingspan

Male: Mostly white with a gray back. Gray upper surface of wings with white edges and black wing tips. Large yellow bill with an orange dot near end of lower mandible. Winter has some fine brown streaking on cap and nape.

Female: same as male

Juvenile: light brown overall with a dark band on the end of tail, dark bill

Nest: ground; female and male construct; 1 brood per year

Eggs: 1-4; light brown without markings

Incubation: 24-29 days; female and male incubate

Fledging: 42-48 days; female and male feed young

Migration: non-migrator; will move up and down the coast to find food during winter

Food: fish, aquatic insects, shellfish

Compare: California Gull (pg. 367) is smaller and has a red and black mark near the tip of lower mandible. The Bonaparte's Gull (pg. 363) is much smaller and has a small black bill.

Stan's Notes: A large gull of rocky shores and coastal cliffs. It has learned to drop shellfish from air onto rocks to break them open. Nests in large colonies with other shorebirds, building a grass nest near water or in a man-made structure. One parent incubates and one stands guard. Performs distraction display to draw danger away from nest. In hot weather, soaks its belly feathers to transport water to cool eggs. A four-year gull, attaining breeding plumage at 4 years.

in flight

SNOWY EGRET
Egretta thula

YEAR-ROUND SUMMER

Size: 24" (60 cm); up to 3½-foot wingspan

Male: All-white bird. Black bill. Black legs. Bright yellow feet. Long feather plumes on head, neck and back during breeding season.

Female: same as male

Juvenile: similar to adult, but backs of legs are yellow

Nest: platform; female and male build; 1 brood per year

Eggs: 3-5; light blue-green without markings

Incubation: 20-24 days; female and male incubate

Fledging: 28-30 days; female and male feed young

Migration: non-migrator to partial in California

Food: aquatic insects, small fish

Compare: Much smaller than Great Egret (pg. 375), which has a yellow bill and black feet. Look for the black bill and yellow feet of Snowy Egret to help identify.

Stan's Notes: Common in wetlands and often seen with other egrets. Colonies may include up to several hundred nests. Nests are low in shrubs 5-10 feet (1.5-3 m) tall or are on the ground, usually mixed among other egret and heron nests. Chicks hatch days apart (asynchronous), leading to starvation of last to hatch. Will actively "hunt" prey by moving around quickly, stirring up small fish and aquatic insects with its feet. In the breeding state, a yellow patch at the base of bill and the yellow feet turn orange-red. Was hunted to near extinction in the late 1800s for its feathers.

371

white
morph

blue morph

juvenile

Ross's Goose

in flight

MIGRATION
WINTER

SNOW GOOSE
Chen caerulescens

Size: 25-38" (63-96 cm); up to 4½-foot wingspan

Male: A mostly white goose with varying patches of black and brown. Black wing tips. Pink bill and legs. Some birds are grayish with a white head.

Female: same as male

Juvenile: overall dull gray with a dark bill

Nest: ground; female builds; 1 brood per year

Eggs: 3-5; white without markings

Incubation: 23-25 days; female incubates

Fledging: 45-49 days; female and male teach young to feed

Migration: complete, to California and Mexico

Food: aquatic insects and plants

Compare: Tundra Swan (pg. 377) is much larger and lacks the black wing tips. Canada Goose (pg. 315) has a black neck and white chin strap. White Pelican (pg. 379) shares black wing tips, but has an enormous bill.

Stan's Notes: Two color morphs. The more common white morph is pure white with black wing tips. Gray morph is often called blue, with a white head, gray chest and back and pink bill and legs. Has a thick serrated bill for pulling up plants. Breeds in large colonies on tundra of northern Canada. Females start breeding at 2-3 years. Older females produce more eggs and are more successful than the younger females. Seen by the thousands during migration and in winter. The Ross's Goose (see inset) is slightly smaller with a much smaller pink bill. Often seen with Ross's Geese and Sandhill Cranes.

in flight

GREAT EGRET
Ardea alba

YEAR-ROUND
MIGRATION
SUMMER

Size: 38" (96 cm); up to 4½-foot wingspan

Male: Tall, thin, elegant all-white bird with long, pointed yellow bill. Black stilt-like legs and black feet.

Female: same as male

Juvenile: same as adult

Nest: platform; male and female build; 1 brood per year

Eggs: 2-3; light blue without markings

Incubation: 23-26 days; female and male incubate

Fledging: 43-49 days; female and male feed young

Migration: complete to non-migrator in California

Food: fish, aquatic insects, frogs, crayfish

Compare: The Snowy Egret (pg. 371) is much smaller with yellow feet and a black bill unlike the black feet and yellow bill of the Great Egret. Great Blue Heron (pg. 319) has a similar shape, but is larger in size and is not white.

Stan's Notes: A tall and stately bird, the Great Egret slowly stalks shallow wetlands looking for small fish to spear with its long sharp bill. Nests in colonies of up to 100 birds. Now protected, they were hunted to near extinction in the 1800s and early 1900s for their long white plumage. The name "Egret" came from the French word *aigrette*, which means "ornamental tufts of plumes." The plumes grow near the tail during breeding season.

juvenile

in flight

TUNDRA SWAN
Cygnus columbianus

Size: 50-54" (127-137 cm); up to 5½-ft. wingspan

Male: Large all-white swan with all-black bill, legs and feet. Has a small yellow mark in front of each eye.

Female: same as male

Juvenile: same size as adult, gray plumage, pinkish gray bill

Nest: ground; female and male construct; 1 brood per year

Eggs: 4-5; creamy white without markings

Incubation: 35-40 days; female and male incubate

Fledging: 60-70 days; female and male feed young

Migration: complete, to parts of California

Food: plants, aquatic insects

Compare: Snow Goose (pg. 373) is much smaller and has black wing tips. Look for Swan's black bill and legs.

Stan's Notes: Nests on the tundra of northern Canada and Alaska, hence its common name. Usually seen during migration and winter. Gathers in large numbers in some lakes and rivers to rest for a day or two before continuing migration. Flies in large V-shaped wedges. Often seen in large family groups of 20 or more individuals. Young are easy to distinguish by their gray plumage and pinkish bills. Gives a high-pitched, whistle-like call.

in flight

chick-feeding
adult

AMERICAN WHITE PELICAN
Pelecanus erythrorhynchos

Size: 62" (158 cm); up to 9-foot wingspan

Male: A large white bird with black wing tips that extend partially down the trailing edge of wings. A white or pale yellow crown. Bright yellow bill, legs and feet. Breeding adult has a bright orange bill and legs. An adult that is feeding chicks (chick-feeding adult) has a gray-black crown.

Female: same as male

Juvenile: duller white with brownish head and neck

Nest: ground, a scraped-out depression rimmed with dirt; female and male build; 1 brood per year

Eggs: 1-3; white without markings

Incubation: 29-36 days; male and female incubate

Fledging: 60-70 days; female and male feed young

Migration: non-migrator in most of California

Food: fish

Compare: Very similar to the Brown Pelican (pg. 239), only white with a yellow or orange bill.

Stan's Notes: Often seen in large groups on the larger lakes and reservoirs of California. They feed by simultaneously dipping their bills into water to scoop up fish. They don't dive in water to catch fish, like coastal Brown Pelicans. Bills and legs of breeding adults turn deep orange. Breeding adults usually also grow a flat fibrous plate in the middle of the upper mandible. This plate drops off after the eggs have hatched. They fly in a large V, often gliding with long wings, then all flapping together.

female

male

WILSON'S WARBLER
Wilsonia pusilla

YEAR-ROUND
MIGRATION
SUMMER

Size: 4¾" (12 cm)

Male: Dull yellow upper and bright yellow lower. Distinctive black cap. Large black eyes and small thin bill.

Female: same as male, but lacking the black cap

Juvenile: similar to female

Nest: cup; female builds; 1 brood per year

Eggs: 4-6; white with brown markings

Incubation: 10-13 days; female incubates

Fledging: 8-11 days; female and male feed young

Migration: complete to non-migrator in California

Food: insects

Compare: Yellow Warbler (pg. 393) is brighter yellow with orange streaking on the male's chest. Male American Goldfinch (pg. 387) has a black forehead and black wings. The male Common Yellowthroat (pg. 389) has a very distinctive black mask.

Stan's Notes: A widespread warbler seen during migration and in summer. Can be found near water in willow and alder thickets. Its all-insect diet makes it one of the top insect-eating birds in North America. Often flicks its tail and spreads its wings when hopping among thick shrubs, looking for insects. Females often mate with males that have the best territories and that might already have mates (polygyny).

male

female

LESSER GOLDFINCH
Carduelis psaltria

Size: 4½" (11 cm)

Male: Striking bright yellow underneath from the chin down to the base of tail. Black cap, tail and wings. Several white patches on wings. Greenish back.

Female: dull yellow below, lacking the black cap

Juvenile: same as female

Nest: cup; female builds; 1-2 broods per year

Eggs: 4-5; pale blue without markings

Incubation: 10-12 days; female incubates

Fledging: 12-14 days; female and male feed young

Migration: partial migrator to non-migrator; will move around the state to find food

Food: seeds, insects; will come to seed feeders

Compare: The male American Goldfinch (pg. 387) is slightly larger and has a yellow back unlike the greenish back of male Lesser Goldfinch. The male Lawrence's Goldfinch (pg. 385) is mostly gray with a black chin.

Stan's Notes: The western males have greenish backs, while males in the eastern range (Texas) have entirely black heads and backs. Some females are extremely pale. Prefers forest edges, areas with short trees and a consistent water source. Unlike many birds, the Lesser Goldfinch's diet is about 96 percent seed, even in peak insect season. Will come to seed feeders. Late summer nesters, male feeds incubating female by regurgitating partially digested seeds. Pairs stay together all winter. Winter flocks can number in the hundreds.

LAWRENCE'S GOLDFINCH
Carduelis lawrencei

YEAR-ROUND
MIGRATION
SUMMER
WINTER

Size: 4¾" (12 cm)

Male: Pale gray bird with bright yellow highlights on breast, wing bars and rump. Black face and chin. Dark wings and tail.

Female: similar to male, not as bright yellow, lacks the black face and chin

Juvenile: similar to female

Nest: cup; female builds; 1-2 broods per year

Eggs: 3-6; pale blue without markings

Incubation: 12-14 days; female and male incubate

Fledging: 11-13 days; male and female feed young

Migration: partial to complete, to southern California and northern Mexico

Food: seeds, insects

Compare: The Lesser Goldfinch (pg. 383) has more yellow and lacks the gray back and black chin of male Lawrence's. The breeding male American Goldfinch (pg. 387) has much more yellow and lacks the male Lawrence's black chin.

Stan's Notes: A finch of wetlands, chaparral and arid areas with water nearby. Strong association with water and plentiful seed crops from native plants. Clings to seed heads and plucks ripe seeds. Also feeds on the ground, taking insects with fallen seeds. Well known for its song, mainly imitations of other bird calls. Returns in April and May to breeding grounds. Usually nests near other Lawrence's. Male feeds nesting female and young. When not breeding, often in flocks with other finches. Frequently seen bathing in shallow water.

male

winter male

female

YEAR-ROUND
WINTER

AMERICAN GOLDFINCH
Carduelis tristis

Size: 5" (13 cm)

Male: A perky yellow bird with a black patch on forehead. Black tail with conspicuous white rump. Black wings with white wing bars. No marking on the chest. Dramatic change in color during winter, similar to female.

Female: dull olive yellow without a black forehead, with brown wings and a white rump

Juvenile: same as female

Nest: cup; female builds; 1 brood per year

Eggs: 4-6; pale blue without markings

Incubation: 10-12 days; female incubates

Fledging: 11-17 days; female and male feed young

Migration: non-migrator to partial; flocks of up to 20 move around North America

Food: seeds, insects; will come to seed feeders

Compare: The male Lesser Goldfinch (pg. 383) has a greenish back. Male Lawrence's (pg. 385) has a black chin. Pine Siskin (pg. 103) and female House Finch (pg. 105) both have streaked chests. The male Wilson's Warbler (pg. 381) lacks black wings. Male Yellow Warbler (pg. 393) has orange on the chest.

Stan's Notes: Most often found in open fields, scrubby areas and woodlands. Often called Wild Canary. A feeder bird that enjoys Nyjer Thistle. Late summer nesting, uses the silky down from wild thistle for nest. Appears roller-coaster-like in flight. Listen for it to twitter during flight. Almost always in small flocks.

male

female

COMMON YELLOWTHROAT
Geothlypis trichas

YEAR-ROUND
SUMMER

Size: 5" (13 cm)

Male: Olive brown bird with bright yellow throat and breast, a white belly and a distinctive black mask outlined in white. A long, thin, pointed black bill.

Female: similar to male, lacks the black mask

Juvenile: same as female

Nest: cup; female builds; 2 broods per year

Eggs: 3-5; white with brown markings

Incubation: 11-12 days; female incubates

Fledging: 10-11 days; female and male feed young

Migration: non-migrator to partial in California

Food: insects

Compare: Found in a similar habitat as the American Goldfinch (pg. 387), but lacks the male's black forehead and wings. The male Yellow Warbler (pg. 393) has fine orange streaks on the breast and lacks male Yellowthroat's mask. Yellow-rumped Warbler (pg. 255) has only spots of yellow. The male Wilson's Warbler (pg. 381) lacks the Yellowthroat's black mask.

Stan's Notes: A common warbler of open fields and marshes. Has a cheerful, well-known song, "witchity-witchity-witchity-witchity." The male performs a curious courtship display, bouncing in and out of tall grass while uttering an unusual song. The young remain dependent upon the parents longer than most warblers. A frequent cowbird host.

ORANGE-CROWNED WARBLER
Vermivora celata

Size: 5" (13 cm)

Male: An overall pale yellow bird with a dark line through eyes. Faint streaking on sides and chest. Small thin bill. Tawny orange crown, often invisible.

Female: same as male, but very slightly duller, often indistinguishable in the field

Juvenile: same as adults

Nest: cup; female builds; 1-2 broods per year

Eggs: 3-6; white with brown markings

Incubation: 12-14 days; female incubates

Fledging: 8-10 days; female and male feed young

Migration: non-migrator to partial in California

Food: insects, fruit, nectar

Compare: Yellow Warbler (pg. 393) is brighter yellow with orange streaking on the male's chest. Wilson's Warbler (pg. 381) is also brighter yellow with a distinct black cap. The male Common Yellowthroat (pg. 389) has a very distinctive black mask.

Stan's Notes: This widespread warbler can be seen year-round in western California. Often seen more during migration when large groups move together. Builds a bulky, well-concealed nest on the ground with nest rim at ground level. Known to feed at sapsucker taps and drink flower nectar. The orange crown tends to be hidden and is rarely seen in the field. A widespread breeder, from western Texas to Alaska and across Canada.

YELLOW WARBLER
Dendroica petechia

SUMMER
WINTER

Size: 5" (13 cm)

Male: Yellow warbler with orange streaks on the chest and belly. Long, pointed dark bill.

Female: same as male, but lacking orange streaking

Juvenile: similar to female, only much duller

Nest: cup; female builds; 1 brood per year

Eggs: 4-5; white with brown markings

Incubation: 11-12 days; female incubates

Fledging: 10-12 days; female and male feed young

Migration: complete, to southern California, Mexico, Central and South America

Food: insects

Compare: Look for orange streaking on chest of male. Orange-crowned Warbler (pg. 391) is paler yellow. Male American Goldfinch (pg. 387) has black wings and forehead. The female Yellow Warbler is similar to the female American Goldfinch (pg. 387), but lacks white wing bars. Similar to male Wilson's Warbler (pg. 381), which has a black cap, and lacks orange streaks on chest and belly.

Stan's Notes: A widespread, common summer warbler in the state, seen in gardens and shrubby areas near water. It is a prolific insect eater, gleaning small caterpillars and other insects from tree leaves. Male is often seen higher up in trees than the female. Female is less conspicuous. Starts to migrate in August and returns in late April. Males arrive 1-2 weeks before females to claim territories. Migrates at night in mixed flocks of warblers. Rests and feeds days.

non-breeding male

breeding male

female

WESTERN TANAGER
Piranga ludoviciana

MIGRATION
SUMMER

Size: 7¼" (18.5 cm)

Male: A canary yellow bird with a red head. Black back, tail, wings. One white and one yellow wing bar. Non-breeding lacks the red head.

Female: duller than male, lacking the red head

Juvenile: similar to female

Nest: cup; female builds; 1 brood per year

Eggs: 3-5; light blue with brown markings

Incubation: 11-13 days; female incubates

Fledging: 13-15 days; female and male feed young

Migration: complete, to Mexico and Central America

Food: insects, fruit

Compare: Male American Goldfinch (pg. 387) has a black forehead and lacks breeding Western male's red head. The female Bullock's Oriole (pg. 397) and Scott's Oriole (pg. 401) lack female Western's single yellow wing bars.

Stan's Notes: The male is stunning in its breeding plumage. Feeds mainly on insects such as bees, wasps, grasshoppers and cicadas. Feeds to a lesser degree on fruit. Male feeds female as she incubates. Female builds a cup nest in a horizontal fork of a coniferous tree, well away from the main trunk, from 20-40 feet (6-12 m) above ground. This is the farthest nesting tanager species, reaching far up into the Northwest Territories of Canada. An early autumn migrant, often seen migrating in late July (when non-breeding males lack red heads). Can be seen in just about any habitat during migration.

male pg. 347

female

SUMMER

BULLOCK'S ORIOLE
Icterus bullockii

Size: 8" (20 cm)

Female: Dull yellow head and chest. Gray-to-black wings with white wing bars. A pale white belly. Gray back, as seen in flight.

Male: bright orange and black, bold white patch on wings

Juvenile: similar to female

Nest: pendulous; female and male build; 1 brood per year

Eggs: 4-6; pale white to gray, brown markings

Incubation: 12-14 days; female incubates

Fledging: 12-14 days; female and male feed young

Migration: complete, to Central and South America

Food: insects, berries, nectar; visits nectar feeders

Compare: Female Scott's Oriole (pg. 401) is larger and lacks the pale white belly. Female Western Tanager (pg. 395) has a black back. Female Hooded (pg. 399) is the same size, but lacks the pale white belly. Look for female Bullock's dull yellow and gray appearance.

Stan's Notes: So closely related to Baltimore Orioles of the eastern U.S., at one time both were considered a single species. Interbreeds with Baltimores where their ranges overlap. Most common in the state where cottonwood trees grow along rivers and other wetlands. Also found at edges of clearings, in city parks, on farms and along irrigation ditches. Hanging sock-like nest is constructed of plant fibers such as inner bark of junipers and willows. Will incorporate yarn and thread into its nest if offered at the time of nest building.

female

male pg. 349

HOODED ORIOLE
Icterus cucullatus

SUMMER

Size:	8" (20 cm)
Female:	A dull yellow head, breast, belly, rump and tail. Gray wings and back. White wing bar. Black eyes.
Male:	orange yellow with black throat, dark wings
Juvenile:	similar to adult of the same sex
Nest:	pendulous; female and male construct; 1-2 broods per year
Eggs:	3-5; dull white with brown markings
Incubation:	12-14 days; female incubates
Fledging:	12-14 days; female and male feed young
Migration:	complete, to Central and South America
Food:	insects, fruit, nectar
Compare:	Female Bullock's Oriole (pg. 397) is very similar, but has a pale white belly. Female Scott's Oriole (pg. 401) is larger with black on the throat and upper breast.

Stan's Notes: A bird of tree-lined creeks and streams, palm groves, mesquite and arid scrub, often near suburbs. Male courts female with bows while hopping around her, singing a soft song. Points his bill skyward (like many birds in the blackbird family). Female will respond with a similar dance. Constructs an unusual sock-like nest, hung from a twig or woven through a palm leaf. Entrance often near the top, but can be on the side. Takes 3-7 days to build nest of wiry green grass, shredded palm leaves or yucca fibers. Some repair and reuse nests. Sips flower nectar, but not like hummingbirds. Often slices into the base of a flower, bypassing its natural entrance. Young are fed a regurgitate of insects and nectar the first 5-7 days of life.

male

female

SCOTT'S ORIOLE
Icterus parisorum

MIGRATION
SUMMER

Size: 9" (22.5 cm)

Male: A black head, neck, back, upper breast and tail with lemon yellow belly, shoulders and rump. Long, pointed, slightly down-curved black bill. Dark eyes. Two white wing bars.

Female: similar to male, but has much less black

Juvenile: grayer than female, yellow under belly only

Nest: pendulous; female builds; 1-2 broods a year

Eggs: 2-4; pale blue with brown markings

Incubation: 14-16 days; female and male incubate

Fledging: 14-16 days; female and male feed young

Migration: complete, to Mexico

Food: insects, fruit, nectar; will come to orange or grapefruit halves and nectar feeders

Compare: The female Bullock's Oriole (pg. 397) has a pale white belly. Male American Goldfinch (pg. 387) is much smaller and has black on the forehead, not on the entire head.

Stan's Notes: Found in open dry areas often associated with yucca and palm. Like other oriole species, female constructs a sock-like pouch that hangs from the end of a thin branch or is woven into a hole in a palm leaf. Populations have increased over the past 100 years due to planting of palm trees. Male is yellow, not orange, like other male orioles. Hunts by gleaning insects and caterpillars from leaves. Uses its long pointed bill to poke holes in bases of flowers to get nectar. Parents feed their young by regurgitating a mixture of insects and fruit. Named after General Winfield Scott, who fought in the Mexican War.

WESTERN KINGBIRD
Tyrannus verticalis

SUMMER

Size: 9" (22.5 cm)

Male: Bright yellow belly and yellow under wings. Gray head and chest, often with white chin. Wings and tail are dark gray to nearly black with white outer edges on tail.

Female: same as male

Juvenile: similar to adult, less yellow and more gray

Nest: cup; female and male build; 1 brood a year

Eggs: 3-4; white with brown markings

Incubation: 18-20 days; female incubates

Fledging: 16-18 days; female and male feed young

Migration: complete, to Central America

Food: insects, berries

Compare: Western Meadowlark (pg. 405) shares the Kingbird's yellow belly, but has a distinctive black V-shaped necklace.

Stan's Notes: A bird of open country, frequently seen sitting on top of the same shrub or fence post. Hunts by watching for crickets, bees, grasshoppers and other insects and flying out to catch them, then returns to perch. Parents teach young how to hunt, bringing wounded insects back to the nest for the young to chase. Returns in March. Builds nest in April, often in a fork of a small single trunk tree. Common in most of California, nesting in trees around farms and homesteads.

WESTERN MEADOWLARK
Sturnella neglecta

YEAR-ROUND

Size: 9" (22.5 cm)

Male: Heavy-bodied bird with a short tail. Yellow chest, brown back and prominent black V-shaped necklace. White outer tail feathers.

Female: same as male

Juvenile: same as adult

Nest: cup, on the ground in dense cover; female builds; 1-2 broods per year

Eggs: 3-5; white with brown markings

Incubation: 13-15 days; female incubates

Fledging: 11-13 days; female and male feed young

Migration: non-migrator to partial migrator

Food: insects, seeds

Compare: Western Kingbird (pg. 403) shares a yellow belly, but lacks the Meadowlark's distinctive black V-shaped necklace. The Horned Lark (pg. 135) is smaller and has a white lower chest and belly.

Stan's Notes: This bird is most common in open country. Named "Meadowlark" because it's a bird of meadows and sings like larks of Europe. Best known for its wonderful song. Not a member of the lark family, it belongs to the blackbird family. Related to blackbirds such as grackles and orioles. Like other blackbird family members, it catches prey by poking its long thin bill into places such as holes in the ground or in tufts of grass, where bugs are hiding. Opening its mouth to create space, the bird extracts insects. Often perches on fence posts. It will quickly dive into tall grass when approached. Conspicuous white markings on sides of its very short, stubby tail.

HELPFUL RESOURCES:

Birder's Bug Book, The. Waldbauer, Gilbert. Cambridge: Harvard University Press, 1998.

Birder's Dictionary. Cox, Randall T. Helena, MT: Falcon Press Publishing, 1996.

Birder's Handbook, The. Ehrlich, Paul R., David S. Dobkin and Darryl Wheye. New York: Simon and Schuster, 1988.

Birds Do It, Too: The Amazing Sex Life of Birds. Harrison, Kit and George H. Harrison. Minocqua, WI: Willow Creek Press, 1997.

Birds of Forest, Yard, and Thicket. Eastman, John. Mechanicsburg, PA: Stackpole Books, 1997.

Birds of North America. Kaufman, Kenn. New York: Houghton Mifflin, 2000.

Blackbirds of the Americas. Orians, Gordon H. Seattle: University of Washington Press, 1985.

California Birds: Their Status and Distribution. Small, Arnold. Vista, CA: Ibis Publishing, 1994.

Cry of the Sandhill Crane, The. Grooms, Steve. Minocqua, WI: NorthWord Press, 1992.

Dictionary of American Bird Names, The. Choate, Ernest A. Boston: Harvard Common Press, 1985.

Everything You Never Learned About Birds. Rupp, Rebecca. Pownal, VT: Storey Publishing, 1997.

Field Guide to the Birds of North America: Third Edition. Washington, DC: National Geographic Society, 1999.

Field Guide to Warblers of North America, A. Dunn, Jon and Kimball Garrett. Boston: Houghton Mifflin, 1997.

Field Guide to Western Birds, A. Peterson, Roger Tory. Boston: Houghton Mifflin, 1998.

Folklore of Birds. Martin, Laura C. Old Saybrook, CT: Globe Pequot Press, 1996.

Guide to Bird Behavior, A: Vol I, II, III. Stokes, Donald and Lillian Stokes. Boston: Little, Brown and Company, 1989.

How Birds Migrate. Kerlinger, Paul. Mechanicsburg, PA: Stackpole Books, 1995.

Lives of Birds, The: Birds of the World and Their Behavior. Short, Lester L. Collingdale, PA: DIANE Publishing, 2000.

Lives of North American Birds. Kaufman, Kenn. Boston: Houghton Mifflin, 1996.

Living on the Wind. Weidensaul, Scott. New York: North Point Press, 2000.

National Audubon Society: North American Birdfeeder Handbook. Burton, Robert. New York: Dorling Kindersley Publishing, 1995.

National Audubon Society: The Sibley Guide to Bird Life and Behavior. Edited by David Allen Sibley, Chris Elphick and John B. Dunning, Jr. New York: Alfred A. Knopf, 2001.

National Audubon Society: The Sibley Guide to Birds. Sibley, David Allen. New York: Alfred A. Knopf, 2000.

Photographic Guide to North American Raptors, A. Wheeler, Brian K. and William S. Clark. New York: Academic Press, 1999.

Secret Lives of Birds, The. Gingras, Pierre. Toronto: Key Porter Books, 1997.

Secrets of the Nest. Dunning, Joan. Boston: Houghton Mifflin, 1994.

Sparrows and Buntings: A Guide to the Sparrows and Buntings of North America and the World. Byers, Clive, Jon Curson and Urban Olsson. New York: Houghton Mifflin, 1995.

Stokes Bluebird Book: The Complete Guide to Attracting Bluebirds. Stokes, Donald and Lillian Stokes. Boston: Little, Brown and Company, 1991.

Stokes Field Guide to Birds: Western Region. Stokes, Donald and Lillian Stokes. Boston: Little, Brown and Company, 1996.

CALIFORNIA BIRDING HOTLINES:

To report unusual bird sightings or possibly hear recordings of where birds have been seen, you can often call pre-recorded hotlines detailing such information. Since these hotlines are usually staffed by volunteers, and phone numbers and even the organizations that host them often change, the phone numbers are not listed here. To obtain the numbers, go to your favorite internet search engine, type in something like "rare bird alert hotline California" and follow the links provided.

WEB PAGES:

The internet is a valuable place to learn more about birds. You may find birding on the net a fun way to discover additional information or to spend a long winter night. These web sites will assist you in your pursuit of birds. If a web address doesn't work (they often change), enter the name of the group into a search engine to track down the new web address.

SITE	ADDRESS
California Bird Records Committee	www.wfo-cbrc.org/cbrc/index.html
American Birding Association	www.americanbirding.org
Cornell Lab of Ornithology	www.birds.cornell.edu
Author Stan Tekiela's home page	www.naturesmart.com

CHECK LIST/INDEX

Use the boxes to check the birds you've seen.

ABOUT THE AUTHOR:

Stan Tekiela is a naturalist, author and wildlife photographer with a Bachelor of Science degree in Natural History from the University of Minnesota. He has been a professional naturalist for more than 20 years and is a member of the Minnesota Naturalist Association, Minnesota Ornithologist Union, Outdoor Writers Association of America, North American Nature Photography Association and Canon Professional Services. Stan actively studies and photographs birds throughout the United States. He has received various national and regional awards for outdoor education and writing. A columnist and radio personality, his syndicated column appears in over 20 cities and he can be heard on a number of radio stations. Stan resides in Victoria, Minnesota, with wife Katherine and daughter Abigail. He can be contacted via his web page at www.naturesmart.com.

Stan authors field guides for other states including guides for birds, birds of prey, mammals, reptiles and amphibians, trees and wildflowers.